# The Modern Stylists

DONALD HALL
EDITOR

# The Modern Stylists

## Writers on the Art of Writing

THE FREE PRESS, NEW YORK
COLLIER-MACMILLAN LIMITED, LONDON

*For M. M. Frohlich*

# A Note to Readers and Users
## of this Book

THE WRITERS assembled here are among the greatest modern writers in our language. Some of the authors here —Fowler most notably—are particularly considerable because of their writing about style.

Although style is not grammar, some grammatical terms and distinctions enter the discussion of style. My assumption in preparing this book is that the reader already writes grammatically, or that he knows where to go for the rules.

The book is not arranged by topic, because I did not wish to chop up such fine essays as those by Orwell and Thurber. Instead, I have provided an Index of Topics at the back of the book. Should a reader want to see what various writers have to say about clichés, or passives, he will find it in the Index.

I have arranged the book to be read straight through, interrupting a succession of longer pieces by interludes of short paragraphs. The short paragraphs contain some of the best writing about style, but many of them defy classification by subject, and so I have placed them largely at random throughout the book. The few that seemed particularly suited to the task, I designated Beginnings and Conclusions. The rest are interludes and make, I hope, some rhythmic division in the form of this book. When I have felt that a particular excerpt might require introduction, I have done so in a footnote. Otherwise I have tried not to intrude.

D. H.

# Contents

*A Note to Readers and Users of this Book*                      *vii*


*Introduction: An Ethic of Clarity*                               *1*

*Beginnings*
    JAMES THURBER                              *11*
    ROBERT GRAVES and ALAN HODGE               *11*
    EZRA POUND                                 *12*

    GEORGE ORWELL
        *"Politics and the English Language"*     *13*

*Interludes 1*
    ERNEST HEMINGWAY                           *31*
    WILLIAM CARLOS WILLIAMS                    *32*
    VIRGINIA WOOLF                             *34*

    ROBERT GRAVES and ALAN HODGE               *37*
        From *The Reader Over Your Shoulder*

*Interludes 2*
    ROBERT FROST                               *57*
    VIRGINIA WOOLF                             *58*
    ERNEST HEMINGWAY                           *59*
    EZRA POUND                                 *59*

EDMUND WILSON
  "Mr. Joseph E. Davies as a Stylist"          66

Interludes 3
  EZRA POUND                                    75
  SIR ARTHUR QUILLER-COUCH                      76
  JAMES THURBER                                 78

  H. W. FOWLER                                  81
    From Modern English Usage

Interludes 4
  E. B. WHITE                                  119
  KATHERINE ANNE PORTER                        121
  MARIANNE MOORE                               123
  GEORGES SIMENON                              123
  MARY McCARTHY                                124
  TRUMAN CAPOTE                                124

  H. L. MENCKEN                                127
    "Euphemisms"

Interludes 5
  ERNEST HEMINGWAY                             145
  GERTRUDE STEIN                               146
  E. B. WHITE                                  149
  WOLCOTT GIBBS                                152

  HERBERT READ                                 155
    From English Prose Style

*Interludes 6*

JAMES THURBER                 173
EZRA POUND                    173
WINSTON CHURCHILL             175

JAMES THURBER
*"The New Vocabularianism"*    177

*Conclusions*

EZRA POUND                    183
ERNEST HEMINGWAY              183

# INTRODUCTION: AN ETHIC OF CLARITY

EZRA POUND, George Orwell, James Thurber, and Ernest Hemingway don't have much in common: a great poet who became a follower of Mussolini, a disillusioned left-wing satirist, a comic essayist and cartoonist, and a great novelist. If anything, they could represent the diversity of modern literature. Yet one thing unites them. They share a common idea of good style, an idea of the virtues of clarity and simplicity. This attitude toward style was not unknown to earlier writers, but never before has it been so pervasive and so exclusive.

Style is the manner of a sentence, not its matter. But the distinction between manner and matter is a slippery one, for manner affects matter. When *Time* used to tell us that President Truman slouched into one room, while General Eisenhower strode into another, their manner was trying to prejudice our feelings. The hotel that invites me to enjoy my favorite beverage at the Crown Room is trying not to sound crass: "Have a drink at the bar." One linguist, in discussing this problem, took Caesar's "I came; I saw; I conquered," and revised it as, "I arrived on the scene of the battle; I observed the situation; I won the victory." Here, the matter is the same, but Caesar's tone of arrogant dignity disappears in the palid pedantry of the longer version. It is impossible to say that the matter is unaffected. But, let us say that this kind of difference, in the two versions of Caesar, is what we mean by style.

1

In the expression "good writing" or "good style," the word "good" has usually meant "beautiful" or "proficient" —like a good Rembrandt or a good kind of soap. In our time it has come to mean honest as opposed to fake. Bad writing happens when the writer lies to himself, to others, or to both. Probably, it is usually necessary to lie to oneself in order to lie to others; advertising men use the products they praise. Bad writing may be proficient; it may persuade us to buy a poor car or vote for an imbecile, but it is bad because it is tricky, false in its enthusiasm, and falsely motivated. It appeals to a part of us that wants to deceive itself. I am encouraged to tell myself that I am enjoying my favorite beverage when, really, I am only getting sloshed.

"If a man writes clearly enough any one can see if he fakes," says Hemingway. Orwell reverses the terms: "The great enemy of clear language is insincerity. . . . When there is a gap between one's real and one's declared aims, one turns as it were instinctively to long words and exhausted idioms, like a cuttlefish squirting out ink." Pound talks about the "gap between one's real and one's declared aims" as the distance between expression and meaning. In "The New Vocabularianism," Thurber speaks of the political use of clichés to hide a "menacing Alice in Wonderland meaninglessness."

As Robert Graves says, "The writing of good English is thus a moral matter." And the morality is a morality of truth-telling. Herbert Read declares that "the only thing that is indispensible for the possession of a good style is personal sincerity." We can agree, but we must add that personal sincerity is not always an easy matter, nor is it always available to the will. Real aims, we must understand, are not necessarily conscious ones. The worst liars in the world may consider themselves sincere. Analysis of one's own style, in fact, can be a test of one's own feelings. And certainly, many habits of bad style are bad habits of thinking as well as of feeling.

There are examples of the modern attitude toward style in older writers. Jonathan Swift, maybe the best prose writer of the language, sounds like George Orwell when he writes:

> . . . Our English tongue is too little cultivated in this kingdom, yet the faults are nine in ten owing to affectation, not to want of understanding. When a man's thoughts are clear, the properest words will generally offer themselves first, and his own judgment will direct him in what order to place them, so as they may be best understood.

Here Swift appears tautological; clear thoughts only *exist* when they are embodied in clear words. But he goes on: "When men err against this method, it is usually on purpose," purposes, we may add, that we often disguise from ourselves.

Aristotle in his *Rhetoric* makes a case for plainness and truth-telling. "The right thing in speaking really is that we should be satisfied not to annoy our hearers, without trying to delight them: we ought in fairness to fight our case with no help beyond the bare facts." And he anticipates the modern stylist's avoidance of unusual words: "Clearness is secured by using the words . . . that are current and ordinary." Cicero attacks the Sophists because they are "on the lookout for ideas that are neatly put rather than reasonable. . . ."

Yet, when we quote Cicero, the master rhetorician, on behalf of honest clarity, we must remember that the ancients did not really think of style as we do. Style until recent times has been a division of rhetoric. To learn style, one learned the types of figures of speech and the appropriateness of each to different levels of discourse—high, middle, and low. The study of style was complex, but it was technical rather than moral. For some writers, Latin was high and the vernacular low, but in the Renaissance the vernacular took in all levels. It is only in modern times that style divorces itself from rhetoric—rhetoric belongs to the enemy, to the advertisers and the propagandists—and becomes a matter of ethics and introspection.

Ezra Pound, like some French writers before him, makes the writer's function social. "Good writers are those who keep the language efficient. That is to say, keep it accurate, keep it clear." We must ask why this idea of the function of good style is so predominantly a modern phenomenon. Pound elsewhere speaks of the "assault," by which he means the attack upon our ears and eyes of words used dishonestly to persuade us, to convince us to buy or to believe. Never before have men been exposed to so many words—written words, from newspapers and billboards and paperbacks and flashing signs and the sides of buses, and spoken words, from radio and television and loudspeakers. Everyone who wishes to keep his mind clear and his feelings his own must make an effort to brush away these words like cobwebs from the face. The assault of the phoney is a result of technology combined with a morality that excuses any technique which is useful for persuasion. The persuasion is for purposes of making money, as in advertising, or winning power, as in war propaganda and the slogans of politicians. Politicians have always had slogans, but they never before had the means to spread their words so widely. The cold war of rhetoric between communism and capitalism has killed no soldiers, but the air is full of the small corpses of words that were once alive: "democracy," "freedom," "liberation."

It is because of this assault, primarily, that writers have become increasingly concerned with the honesty of their style to the exclusion of other qualities. Concentration on honesty is the only way to exclude the sounds of the bad style that assault us all. These writers are concerned finally *to be honest about what they see, feel, and know.* For some of them, like William Carlos Williams, we can only trust the evidence of our eyes and ears, our real knowledge of our immediate environment.

Our reading of good writers and our attempt to write like them can help to guard us against the dulling onslaught. But we can only do this if we are able to look into ourselves with some honesty. An ethic of clarity demands intelligence and self-knowledge. Really, the ethic is not only a defense against the assault (nothing good is ever merely defensive), but is a development of the same inwardness that is reflected in psychoanalysis. One cannot, after all, examine one's motives and feelings carefully if one takes a naïve view that the appearance of a feeling is the reality of that feeling.

Sometimes, the assault is merely pompous. Some people say "wealthy" instead of "rich" in order to seem proper, or "home" instead of "house" in order to seem genteel. George Orwell translates a portion of *Ecclesiastes* into academic-pompous, for example; Quiller-Couch does something similar with Hamlet's soliloquy. Years ago, James Russell Lowell ridiculed the newspapers that translated "A great crowd came to see . . ." into "A vast concourse was assembled to witness. . . ." None of these examples is so funny as a colonel's statement on television that one of our astronauts "has established visual contact" with a piece of his equipment. He meant that the astronaut had *seen* it.

Comic as these pomposities are, they are signs that something has gone wrong somewhere. (My father normally spoke a perfectly good plain English, but, occasionally, when he was unhappy with himself, he would fall off dreadfully; I remember him once admonishing me at dinner, "It is necessary to masticate thoroughly.") The colonel must have been worried about the intellectual respectability of the space program when he resorted to phrases like "visual contact." The lady who speaks of "luncheon" instead of "lunch" is worried about her social status. She gives herself away. Something has gone wrong, and it has gone wrong inside her mind and her emotions.

The style is the man. Again and again, the modern stylists repeat this idea. By a man's metaphors you shall know him. When a commencement orator advises students to enrich themselves culturally, chances are that he is more interested in money than in poetry. When a university president says that his institution turned out 1,432 B.A.s last year, he tells us that he thinks he is running General Motors. The style is the man. Remy de Gourmont used the analogy that the bird's song is conditioned by the shape of the beak. And Paul Valery said, ". . . what makes

5

the style is not merely the mind applied to a particular action; it is the whole of a living system extended, imprinted and recognizable in expression." These statements are fine, but they sound too deterministic, as if one expresses an unalterable self and can no more change the style of that self than a bird can change the shape of its beak. Man is a kind of bird that can change his beak.

A writer of bad prose, to become a writer of good prose, must alter his character. He does not have to become good in terms of conventional morality, but he must become honest in the expression of himself, which means that he must know himself. There must be no gap between expression and meaning, between real and declared aims. For some people, some of the time, this simply means *not* telling deliberate lies. For most people, it means learning when they are lying and when they are not. It means learning the real names of their feelings. It means not saying or thinking, "I didn't *mean* to hurt your feelings," when there really existed a desire to hurt. It means not saying "luncheon" or "home" for the purpose of appearing upper-class or well-educated. It means not using the passive mood to attribute to no one in particular opinions that one is unwilling to call one's own. It means not disguising banal thinking by polysyllabic writing or the lack of feeling by clichés that purport to display feeling.

The style is the man, and the man can change himself by changing his style. Prose style is the way you think and the way you understand what you feel. Frequently, we feel for one another a mixture of strong love and strong hate; if we call it love and disguise the hate to ourselves by sentimentalizing over love, we are thinking and feeling badly. Style is ethics and psychology; clarity is a psychological sort of ethic, since it involves not general moral laws, but truth to the individual self. The scrutiny of style is a moral and psychological study. By trying to scrutinize our own style, perhaps with the help of people like Orwell and Pound, Hemingway and Thurber, we try to understand ourselves. Editing our own writing, or going over in memory our own spoken words, or even inwardly examining our thought, we can ask *why* we resorted to the passive in this case or to clichés in that. When the smoke of bad prose fills the air, something is always on fire somewhere. If the style is really the man, the style becomes an instrument for discovering and changing the man. Language is expression of self, but language is also the instrument by which to know that self.

D. H.

# *Beginnings*

Here are some of the premises of modern style. James Thurber quotes his old editor on everyone's ignorance of English. Robert Graves and Alan Hodge set forth some basic ideas for every would-be writer. Ezra Pound tersely names the foundations of his thought about style.

# JAMES THURBER

I told him that I wanted to write, and he snarled, "Writers are a dime a dozen, Thurber. What I want is an editor. I can't find editors. Nobody grows up. Do you know English?" I said I thought I knew English, and this started him off on a subject with which I was to become intensely familiar. "Everybody thinks he knows English," he said, "but nobody does. I think it's because of the goddam women schoolteachers."

# ROBERT GRAVES and ALAN HODGE

THERE is not, and cannot be, any permanent model of literary English; but there are everywhere obvious differences between written and spoken English. A speaker reinforces his meaning with gestures and vocal inflexions, and if the people he addresses still do not understand they can ask for further explanation; whereas a writer, not enjoying either of these advantages, must formulate and observe certain literary principles if he wishes to be completely understood. Granted, he may not always wish to be so understood: a good deal of play is made in English with deliberate looseness of phrase. But the only relevant standard by which to judge any straightforward piece of prose is the ease with which it conveys its full intended sense to the readers to whom it is addressed, rather than its correctness by the laws of formal English grammar.

\*
\*
\*

There is an instinctive mistrust of grammarians in Britain and the United States, and a pride in following one's natural course in writing. Deliberate obscurity is rare. We suggest that whenever anyone sits down to write he should imagine a crowd of his prospective readers (rather than a grammarian in cap and gown) looking over his shoulder. They will be asking such questions as "What does this sentence mean?" "Why do you trouble to tell me that again?" "Why have you chosen such a ridiculous metaphor?" "Must I really read this long, limping sentence?" "Haven't you got your ideas muddled here?" By anticipating and listing as many questions of this sort as possible, the writer will discover certain tests of intelligibility to which he may regularly submit his work before he sends it off to the printer.

# EZRA POUND

MORE writers fail from lack of character than from lack of intelligence.

Technical solidity is not attained without at least some persistence.

[From *The ABC of Reading*. All rights reserved. Reprinted by perimission of New Directions Publishing Corporation and Faber & Faber Ltd.]

# George Orwell

## POLITICS AND THE ENGLISH LANGUAGE

MOST people who bother with the matter at all would admit that the English language is in a bad way, but it is generally assumed that we cannot by conscious action do anything about it. Our civilization is decadent and our language—so the argument runs—must inevitably share in the general collapse. It follows that any struggle against the abuse of language is a sentimental archaism, like preferring candles to electric light or hansom cabs to aeroplanes. Underneath this lies the half-conscious belief that language is a natural growth and not an instrument which we shape for our own purposes.

Now, it is clear that the decline of a language must ultimately have political and economic causes: it is not due simply to the bad influence of this or that individual writer. But an effect can become a cause, reinforcing the original cause and producing the same effect in an intensified form, and so on indefinitely. A man may take to drink because he feels himself to be a failure, and then fail all the more completely because he drinks. It is rather the same thing that is happening to the English language. It becomes ugly and inaccurate because our thoughts are foolish, but the slovenliness of our language makes it easier for us to have foolish thoughts. The point is that the process is reversible. Modern English, especially written English, is full of bad habits which spread by imitation and which can be avoided if one is willing to take the necessary trouble. If one gets rid of these habits one can think more clearly, and to think clearly is a necessary first step towards political regeneration: so that the fight against bad English is not frivolous and is not the exclusive concern of professional writers. I will come back to this presently, and I hope that by that time the meaning of what I have said here will have become clearer. Meanwhile, here are five specimens of the English language as it is now habitually written.

These five passages have not been picked out because they are especially bad—I could have quoted far worse if I had chosen—but because they illustrate various of the mental vices from which we now suffer. They are a little below the average, but are fairly representative samples. I number them so that I can refer back to them when necessary:

(1) I am not, indeed, sure whether it is not true to say that the Milton who once seemed not unlike a seventeenth-century Shelley had not become, out of an experience ever more bitter in each year, more alien [sic] to the founder of that Jesuit sect which nothing could induce him to tolerate.

Professor Harold Laski
(Essay in *Freedom of Expression*).

(2) Above all, we cannot play ducks and drakes with a native battery of idioms which prescribes such egregious collocations of vocables as the Basic *put up with* for *tolerate* or *put at a loss* for *bewilder*.

Professor Lancelot Hogben (*Interglossa*).

(3) On the one side we have the free personality: by definition it is not neurotic, for it has neither conflict nor dream. Its desires, such as they are, are transparent, for they are just what institutional approval keeps in the forefront of consciousness; another institutional pattern would alter their number and intensity, there is little in them that is natural, irreducible, or culturally dangerous. But *on the other side*, the social bond itself is nothing but the mutual reflection of these self-secure integrities. Recall the definition of love. Is not this the very

14

picture of a small academic? Where is there a place in this hall
of mirrors for either personality or fraternity?

Essay on psychology in Politics (New York).

(4) All the "best people" from the gentlemen's clubs, and
all the frantic fascist captains, united in common hatred of
Socialism and bestial horror of the rising tide of the mass revolutionary movement, have turned to acts of provocation, to foul
incendiarism, to medieval legends of poisoned wells, to legalize
their own destruction of proletarian organizations, and rouse
the agitated petty-bourgeoisie to chauvinistic fervor on behalf
of the fight against the revolutionary way out of the crisis.

Communist pamphlet.

(5) If a new spirit is to be infused into this old country,
there is one thorny and contentious reform which must be
tackled, and that is the humanization and galvanization of the
B.B.C. Timidity here will bespeak canker and atrophy of the
soul. The heart of Britain may be sound and of strong beat, for
instance, but the British lion's roar at present is like that of Bot-
tom in Shakespeare's *Midsummer Night's Dream*—as gentle as
any sucking dove. A virile new Britain cannot continue indefinitely to be traduced in the eyes, or rather ears, of the world
by the effete languors of Langham Place, brazenly masquerad-
ing as "standard English." When the Voice of Britain is heard
at nine o'clock, better far and infinitely less ludicrous to hear
aitches honestly dropped than the present priggish, inflated, in-
hibited, school-ma'amish arch braying of blameless bashful
mewing maidens!

Letter in Tribune.

Each of these passages has faults of its own, but, quite
apart from avoidable ugliness, two qualities are common
to all of them. The first is staleness of imagery; the other is
lack of precision. The writer either has a meaning and cannot express it, or he inadvertently says something else, or
he is almost indifferent as to whether his words mean anything or not. This mixture of vagueness and sheer incompetence is the most marked chracteristic of modern English
prose, and especially of any kind of political writing. As
soon as certain topics are raised, the concrete melts into the
abstract and no one seems able to think of turns of speech
that are not hackneyed: prose consists less and less of

*words* chosen for the sake of their meaning, and more and more of *phrases* tacked together like the sections of a prefabricated hen-house. I list below, with notes and examples, various of the tricks by means of which the work of prose-construction is habitually dodged:

DYING METAPHORS

A newly invented metaphor assists thought by evoking a visual image, while on the other hand a metaphor which is technically "dead" (e.g. *iron resolution*) has in effect reverted to being an ordinary word and can generally be used without loss of vividness. But in between these two classes there is a huge dump of worn-out metaphors which have lost all evocative power and are merely used because they save people the trouble of inventing phrases for themselves. Examples are: *Ring the changes on, take up the cudgels for, toe the line, ride roughshod over, stand shoulder to shoulder with, play into the hands of, no axe to grind, grist to the mill, fishing in troubled waters, on the order of the day, Achilles' heel, swan song, hotbed.* Many of these are used without knowledge of their meaning (what is a "rift," for instance?), and incompatible metaphors are frequently mixed, a sure sign that the writer is not interested in what he is saying. Some metaphors now current have been twisted out of their original meaning without those who use them even being aware of the fact. For example, *toe the line* is sometimes written *tow the line*. Another example is *the hammer and the anvil*, now always used with the implication that the anvil gets the worst of it. In real life it is always the anvil that breaks the hammer, never the other way about: a writer who stopped to think what he was saying would be aware of this, and would avoid perverting the original phrase.

16

GEORGE ORWELL

OPERATORS OR VERBAL FALSE LIMBS

These save the trouble of picking out appropriate verbs and nouns, and at the same time pad each sentence with extra syllables which give it an appearance of symmetry. Characteristic phrases are *render inoperative, militate against, make contact with, be subjected to, give rise to, give grounds for, have the effect of, play a leading part (role) in, make itself felt, take effect, exhibit a tendency to, serve the purpose of,* etc., etc. The keynote is the elimination of simple verbs. Instead of being a single word, such as *break, stop, spoil, mend, kill,* a verb becomes a *phrase,* made up of a noun or adjective tacked on to some general-purposes verb such as *prove, serve, form, play, render.* In addition, the passive voice is wherever possible used in preference to the active, and noun constructions are used instead of gerunds (*by examination of* instead of *by examining*). The range of verbs is further cut down by means of the *-ize* and *de-* formations, and the banal statements are given an appearance of profundity by means of the *not un-* formation. Simple conjunctions and prepositions are replaced by such phrases as *with respect to, having regard to, the fact that, by dint of, in view of, in the interests of, on the hypothesis that;* and the ends of sentences are saved by anticlimax by such resounding common-places as *greatly to be desired, cannot be left out of account, a development to be expected in the near future, deserving of serious consideration, brought to a satisfactory conclusion* and so on and so forth.

PRETENTIOUS DICTION

Words like *phenomenon, element, individual* (as noun), *objective, categorical, effective, virtual, basic, primary, promote, constitute, exhibit, exploit, utilize, eliminate, liquidate,* are used to dress up simple statement and give an air of scientific impartiality to biased judgments. Adjectives like *epoch-making, epic, historic, unforgettable, trium-*

*phant, age-old, inevitable, inexorable, veritable,* are used to dignify the sordid processes of international politics, while writing that aims at glorifying war usually takes on an archaic color, its characteristic words being: *realm, throne, chariot, mailed fist, trident, sword, shield, buckler, banner, jackboot, clarion.* Foreign words and expressions such as *cul de sac, ancien régime, deus ex machina, mutatis mutandis, status quo, gleichschaltung, weltanschauung,* are used to give an air of culture and elegance. Except for the useful abbreviations *i.e., e.g.,* and *etc.,* there is no real need for any of the hundreds of foreign phrases now current in English. Bad writers, and especially scientific, political and sociological writers, are nearly always haunted by the notion that Latin or Greek words are grander than Saxon ones, and unnecessary words like *expedite, ameliorate, predict, extraneous, deracinated, clandestine, subaqueous* and hundreds of others constantly gain ground from their Anglo-Saxon opposite numbers.[1] The jargon peculiar to Marxist writing (*hyena, hangman, cannibal, petty bourgeois, these gentry, lacquey, flunkey, mad dog, White Guard,* etc.) consists largely of words and phrases translated from Russian, German or French; but the normal way of coining a new word is to use a Latin or Greek root with the appropriate affix and, where necessary, the size formation. It is often easier to make up words of this kind (*deregionalize, impermissible, extramarital, non-fragmentary* and so forth) than to think up the English words that will cover one's meaning. The result, is general, is an increase in slovenliness and vagueness.

1. An interesting illustration of this is the way in which the English flower names which were in use till very recently are being ousted by Greek ones, *snapdragon* becoming *antirrhinum, forget-me-not* becoming *myosotis,* etc. It is hard to see any practical reason for this change of fashion: it is probably due to an instinctive turning-away from the more homely word and a vague feeling that the Greek word is scientific.
2. Example: "Comfort's catholicity of perception and image, strangely Whitmanesque in range, almost the exact opposite in aesthetic

## MEANINGLESS WORDS

In certain kinds of writing, particularly in art criticism and literary criticism, it is normal to come across long passages which are almost completely lacking in meaning.[2] Words like *romantic, plastic, values, human, dead, sentimental, natural, vitality,* as used in art criticism, are strictly meaningless, in the sense that they not only do not point to any discoverable object, but are hardly ever expected to do so by the reader. When one critic writes, "The outstanding feature of Mr. X's work is its living quality," while another writes, "The immediately striking thing about Mr. X's work is its peculiar deadness," the reader accepts this as a simple difference of opinion. If words like *black* and *white* were involved, instead of the jargon words *dead* and *living,* he would see at once that language was being used in an improper way. Many political words are similarly abused. The word *Fascism* has now no meaning except in so far as it signifies "something not desirable." The words *democracy, socialism, freedom, patriotic, realistic, justice,* have each of them several different meanings which cannot be reconciled with one another. In the case of a word like *democracy,* not only is there no agreed definition, but the attempt to make one is resisted from all sides. It is almost universally felt that when we call a country democratic we are praising it: consequently the defenders of every kind of régime claim that it is a democracy, and fear that they might have to stop using the word if it were tied down to any one meaning. Words of this kind are often used in a consciously dishonest way. That is, the person who uses them has his own private definition, but allows his hearer to think he means something quite

---

compulsion, continues to evoke that trembling atmospheric accumulative hinting at a cruel, an inexorably serene timelessness. . . . Wrey Gardiner scores by aiming at simple bull's-eyes with precision. Only they are not so simple, and through this contented sadness runs more than the surface bitter-sweet of resignation." (Poetry Quarterly.)

different. Statements like *Marshal Pétain was a true patriot*, *The Soviet Press is the freest in the world*, *The Catholic Church is opposed to persecution*, are almost always made with intent to deceive. Other words used in variable meanings, in most cases more or less dishonestly, are: *class, totalitarian, science, progressive, reactionary, bourgeois, equality.*

Now that I have made this catalogue of swindles and perversions, let me give another example of the kind of writing that they lead to. This time it must of its nature be an imaginary one. I am going to translate a passage of good English into modern English of the worst sort. Here is a well-known verse from *Ecclesiastes:*

> I returned and saw under the sun, that the race is not to the swift, nor the battle to the strong, neither yet bread to the wise, nor yet riches to men of understanding, nor yet favour to men of skill; but time and chance happeneth to them all.

Here it is in modern English:

> Objective consideration of contemporary phenomena compels the conclusion that success or failure in competitive activities exhibits no tendency to be commensurate with innate capacity, but that a considerable element of the unpredictable must invariably be taken into account.

This is a parody, but not a very gross one. Exhibit (3), above, for instance, contains several patches of the same kind of English. It will be seen that I have not made a full translation. The beginning and ending of the sentence follow the original meaning fairly closely, but in the middle the concrete illustrations—race, battle, bread —dissolve into the vague phrase "success or failure in competitive activities." This had to be so, because no modern writer of the kind I am discussing—no one capable of using phrases like "objective consideration of contemporary phenomena"—would ever tabulate his thoughts in that precise and detailed way. The whole tendency of modern prose is away from concreteness. Now analyse these two sentences a little more closely. The first contains forty-nine words but only sixty syllables, and all its words

20

are those of everyday life. The second contains thirty-eight words of ninety syllables: eighteen of its words are from Latin roots, and one from Greek. The first sentence contains six vivid images, and only one phrase ("time and chance") that could be called vague. The second contains not a single fresh, arresting phrase, and in spite of its ninety syllables it gives only a shortened version of the meaning contained in the first. Yet without a doubt it is the second kind of sentence that is gaining ground in modern English. I do not want to exaggerate. This kind of writing is not yet universal, and outcrops of simplicity will occur here and there in the worst-written page. Still, if you or I were told to write a few lines on the uncertainty of human fortunes, we should probably come much nearer to my imaginary sentence than to the one from *Ecclesiastes*.

As I have tried to show, modern writing at its worst does not consist in picking out words for the sake of their meaning and inventing images in order to make the meaning clearer. It consists in gumming together long strips of words which have already been set in order by someone else, and making the results presentable by sheer humbug. The attraction of this way of writing is that it is easy. It is easier—even quicker, once you have the habit—to say *In my opinion it is not an unjustifiable assumption that* than to say *I think*. If you use ready-made phrases, you not only don't have to hunt about for words; you also don't have to bother with the rhythms of your sentences, since these phrases are generally so arranged as to be more or less euphonious. When you are composing in a hurry—when you are dictating to a stenographer, for instance, or making a public speech—it is natural to fall into a pretentious, Latinized style. Tags like a *consideration which we should do well to bear in mind* or *a conclusion to which all of us would readily assent* will save many a sentence from coming down with a bump. By using stale metaphors, similes and idioms, you save much mental effort, at the cost of leaving your meaning vague, not only for your reader but for yourself.

This is the significance of mixed metaphors. The sole aim of a metaphor is to call up a visual image. When these images clash—as in *The Fascist octopus has sung its swan song, the jackboot is thrown into the melting pot*—it can be taken as certain that the writer is not seeing a mental image of the objects he is naming; in other words he is not really thinking. Look again at the examples I gave at the beginning of this essay. Professor Laski (1) uses five negatives in fifty-three words. One of these is superfluous, making nonsense of the whole passage, and in addition there is the slip *alien* for akin, making further nonsense, and several avoidable pieces of clumsiness which increase the general vagueness. Professor Hogben (2) plays ducks and drakes with a battery which is able to write prescriptions, and, while disapproving of the everyday phrase *put up with*, is unwilling to look *egregious* up in the dictionary and see what it means; (3), if one takes an uncharitable attitude towards it, is simply meaningless: probably one could work out its intended meaning by reading the whole of the article in which it occurs. In (4), the writer knows more or less what he wants to say, but an accumulation of stale phrases chokes him, like tea leaves blocking a sink. In (5), words and meaning have almost parted company. People who write in this manner usually have a general emotional meaning—they dislike one thing and want to express solidarity with another—but they are not interested in the detail of what they are saying. A scrupulous writer, in every sentence that he writes, will ask himself at least four questions, thus: What am I trying to say? What words will express it? What image or idiom will make it clearer? Is this image fresh enough to have an effect? And he will probably ask himself two more: Could I put it more shortly? Have I said anything that is avoidably ugly? But you are not obliged to go to all this trouble. You can shirk it by simply throwing your mind open and letting the ready-made phrases come crowding in. They will construct your sentences for you—even think your thoughts for you, to a certain extent—and at need they will perform the important service of partially concealing your meaning

even from yourself. It is at this point that the special connection between politics and the debasement of language
becomes clear.

In our time it is broadly true that political writing is
bad writing. Where it is not true, it will generally be found
that the writer is some kind of rebel, expressing his private
opinions and not a "party line." Orthodoxy, of whatever
color, seems to demand a lifeless, imitative style. The
political dialects to be found in pamphlets, leading articles,
manifestos, White Papers and the speeches of under-
secretaries do, of course, vary from party to party, but
they are all alike in that one almost never finds in them a
fresh, vivid, home-made turn of speech. When one watches
some tired hack on the platform mechanically repeating the
familiar phrases—*bestial atrocities, iron heel, bloodstained
tyranny, free peoples of the world, stand shoulder to
shoulder*—one often has a curious feeling that one is not
watching a live human being but some kind of dummy: a
feeling which suddenly becomes stronger at moments when
the light catches the speaker's spectacles and turns them
into blank discs which seem to have no eyes behind them.
And this is not altogether fanciful. A speaker who uses
that kind of phraseology has gone some distance towards
turning himself into a machine. The appropriate noises
are coming out of his larynx, but his brain is not involved
as it would be if he were choosing his words for himself.
If the speech he is making is one that he is accustomed
to make over and over again, he may be almost unconscious of what he is saying, as one is when one utters the
responses in church. And this reduced state of consciousness, if not indispensable, is at any rate favorable to political conformity.

In our time, political speech and writing are largely
the defence of the indefensible. Things like the continu-
ance of British rule in India, the Russian purges and depor-
tations, the dropping of the atom bombs on Japan, can
indeed be defended, but only by arguments which are too
brutal for most people to face, and which do not square
with the professed aims of political parties. Thus political

language has to consist largely of euphemism, question-begging and sheer cloudy vagueness. Defenceless villages are bombarded from the air, the inhabitants driven out into the countryside, the cattle machine-gunned, the huts set on fire with incendiary bullets: this is called *pacification*. Millions of peasants are robbed of their farms and sent trudging along the roads with no more than they can carry: this is called *transfer of population* or *rectification of frontiers*. People are imprisoned for years without trial, or shot in the back of the neck or sent to die of scurvy in Arctic lumber camps; this is called *elimination of unreliable elements*. Such phraseology is needed if one wants to name things without calling up mental pictures of them. Consider for instance some comfortable English professor defending Russian totalitarianism. He cannot say outright, "I believe in killing off your opponents when you can get good results by doing so." Probably, therefore, he will say something like this:

"While freely conceding that the Soviet régime exhibits certain features which the humanitarian may be inclined to deplore, we must, I think, agree that a certain curtailment of the right to political opposition is an unavoidable concomitant of transitional periods, and that the rigors which the Russian people have been called upon to undergo have been amply justified in the sphere of concrete achievement."

The inflated style is itself a kind of euphemism. A mass of Latin words falls upon the facts like soft snow, blurring the outlines and covering up all the details. The great enemy of clear language is insincerity. When there is a gap between one's real and one's declared aims, one turns as it were instinctively to long words and exhausted idioms, like a cuttlefish squirting out ink. In our age there is no such thing as "keeping out of politics." All issues are political issues, and politics itself is a mass of lies, evasions, folly, hatred and schizophrenia. When the general atmosphere is bad, language must suffer. I should expect to find—this is a guess which I have not sufficient knowledge to verify—that the German, Russian and Italian languages have all deteriorated in the last ten or fifteen years, as a result of dictatorship.

But if thought corrupts language, language can also corrupt thought. A bad usage can spread by tradition and imitation, even among people who should and do know better. The debased language that I have been discussing is in some ways very convenient. Phrases like *a not unjustifiable assumption, leaves much to be desired, would serve no good purpose, a consideration which we should do well to bear in mind,* are a continuous temptation, a packet of aspirins always at one's elbow. Look back through this essay, and for certain you will find that I have again and again committed the very faults I am protesting against. By this morning's post I have received a pamphlet dealing with conditions in Germany. The author tells me that he "felt impelled" to write it. I open it at random, and here is almost the first sentence that I see: "[The Allies] have an opportunity not only of achieving a radical transformation of Germany's social and political structure in such a way as to avoid a nationalistic reaction in Germany itself, but at the same time of laying the foundations of a co-operative and unified Europe." You see, he "feels impelled" to write—feels, presumably, that he has something new to say—and yet his words, like cavalry horses answering the bugle, group themselves automatically into the familiar dreary pattern. This invasion of one's mind by ready-made phrases (*lay the foundations, achieve a radical transformation*) can only be prevented if one is constantly on guard against them, and every such phrase anaethetizes a portion of one's brain.

I said earlier that the decadence of our language is probably curable. Those who deny this would argue, if they produced an argument at all, that language merely reflects existing social conditions, and that we cannot influence its development by any direct tinkering with words and constructions. So far as the general tone or spirit of a language goes, this may be true, but it is not true in detail. Silly words and expressions have often disappeared, not through any evolutionary process but owing to the conscious action of a minority. Two recent examples were *explore every avenue* and *leave no stone unturned,* which were killed by the jeers of a few journalists. There is a long list of flyblown metaphors which could similarly be got rid of if enough people would interest themselves in the job; and it should also be possible to laugh the *not un-* formation out of existence,[3] to reduce the amount of Latin and Greek in the average sentence, to drive out foreign phrases and strayed scientific words, and, in general, to make pretentiousness unfashionable. But all these are minor points. The defence of the English language implies more than this, and perhaps it is best to start by saying what it does *not* imply.

To begin with it has nothing to do with archaism, with the salvaging of obsolete words and turns of speech, or with the setting up of a "standard English" which must never be departed from. On the contrary, it is especially concerned with the scrapping of every word or idiom which has outworn its usefulness. It has nothing to do with correct grammar and syntax, which are of no importance so long as one makes one's meaning clear, or with the avoidance of Americanisms, or with having what is called a "good prose style." On the other hand it is not concerned with fake simplicity and the attempt to make written English colloquial. Nor does it even imply in every case preferring the Saxon word to the Latin one, though it does imply using the fewest and shortest words that will cover one's meaning. What is above all needed is to let the meaning choose the word, and not the other way about. In prose, the worst thing one can do with words is to surrender to them. When you think of a concrete object, you think wordlessly, and then, if you want to describe the thing you have been visualizing you probably hunt about till you find the exact words that seem to fit it. When you think of something abstract you are more inclined to use words from the start, and unless you make

3. One can cure oneself of the *not un-* formation by memorizing this sentence: *A not unblack dog was chasing a not unsmall rabbit across a not ungreen field.*

26

a conscious effort to prevent it, the existing dialect will come rushing in and do the job for you, at the expense of blurring or even changing your meaning. Probably it is better to put off using words as long as possible and get one's meaning as clear as one can through pictures or sensations. Afterwards one can choose—not simply *accept* —the phrases that will best cover the meaning, and then switch round and decide what impression one's words are likely to make on another person. This last effort of the mind cuts out all stale or mixed images, all prefabricated phrases, needless repetitions, and humbug and vagueness generally. But one can often be in doubt about the effect of a word or a phrase, and one needs rules that one can rely on when instinct fails. I think the following rules will cover most cases:

(i) Never use a metaphor, simile or other figure of speech which you are used to seeing in print.

(ii) Never use a long word where a short one will do.

(iii) If it is possible to cut a word out, always cut it out.

(iv) Never use the passive where you can use the active.

(v) Never use a foreign phrase, a scientific word or a jargon word if you can think of an everyday English equivalent.

(vi) Break any of these rules sooner than say anything outright barbarous.

These rules sound elementary, and so they are, but they demand a deep change of attitude in anyone who has grown used to writing in the style now fashionable. One could keep all of them and still write bad English, but one could not write the kind of stuff that I quoted in those five specimens at the beginning of this article.

I have not here been considering the literary use of language, but merely language as an instrument for expressing and not for concealing or preventing thought. Stuart Chase and others have come near to claiming that all abstract words are meaningless, and have used this as a pretext for advocating a kind of political quietism. Since you don't know what Fascism is, how can you struggle against Fascism? One need not swallow such absurdities as this, but one ought to recognize that the present political chaos is connected with the decay of language, and that one can probably bring about some improvement by starting at the verbal end. If you simplify your English, you are freed from the worst follies of orthodoxy. You cannot speak any of the necessary dialects, and when you make a stupid remark its stupidity will be obvious, even to yourself. Political language—and with variations this is true of all political parties, from Conservatives to Anarchists—is designed to make lies sound truthful and murder respectable, and to give an appearance of solidity to pure wind. One cannot change this all in a moment, but one can at least change one's own habits, and from time to time one can even, if one jeers loudly enough, send some worn-out and useless phrase—some *jackboot, Achilles' heel, hotbed, melting pot, acid test, veritable inferno* or other lump of verbal refuse—into the dustbin where it belongs.

1946

# *Interludes*

# *1*

Ernest Hemingway and William Carlos Williams attack fuzziness and praise clarity of language. Virginia Woolf sets forth examples of good and bad writing, and names some of the premises of good style.

# ERNEST HEMINGWAY

THIS too to remember. If a man writes clearly enough any one can see if he fakes. If he mystifies to avoid a straight statement, which is very different from breaking so-called rules of syntax of grammar to make an effect which can be obtained in no other way, the writer takes a longer time to be known as a fake and other writers who are afflicted by the same necessity will praise him in their own defense. True mysticism should not be confused with incompetence in writing which seeks to mystify where there is no mystery but is really only the necessity to fake to cover lack of knowledge or the inability to state clearly. Mysticism implies a mystery and there are many mysteries; but incompetence is not one of them; nor is overwritten journalism made literature by the injection of a false epic quality. Remember this too: all bad writers are in love with the epic.

*
*
*

. . . Books like Richard Ford's have never had the popularity of the bedside mysticism of such a book as *Virgin Spain*. The author of this book once published a piece in a now dead little magazine called *S4N* explaining how he did his writing. Any historian of letters wanting to explain certain phenomena of our writing can look it up in the files of that magazine. My copy is in Paris or I could quote it in full, but the gist of it was how this writer lay naked in his bed in the night and God sent him things to write, how he "was in touch ecstatically with the plunging and immobile all." How he was, through the courtesy of

God, *"everywhere* and *everywhen."* The italics are his or
maybe they are God's. It didn't say in the article. After
God sent it he wrote it. The result was that unavoidable
mysticism of a man who writes a language so badly he
cannot make a clear statement, complicated by whatever
pseudo-scientific jargon is in style at the moment.

# WILLIAM CARLOS WILLIAMS

MY BROTHER, who is an architect, told me recently that
his mind had been aflame over the problems of construction today more than ever before. Upon what shall we base
our judgments? he said to me almost in despair. You are
a writer, he said, I'd like to know how you work. What
do you find to be of importance? We must both be looking
for more or less the same things. Tell me how you go
about it.

I just sit down and write.

It must be more conscious than that. You must have
some basis for acceptance of a word, a phrase—a general
character of composition. I, for instance, after a lifetime
of practice, feel that I'm just beginning to sense a few of
the underlying movements, call them rules, governing my
profession and that all this talk of "old" and "modern"
has very little to do with the matter.

That's a large piece of woods, though, to get lost in.

The basis is honesty in construction, that you can do
certain things with the material and other things you cannot do. Therein lie all answers.

*
*
*

You know how I started to write, I said. I didn't know
what I was doing but I knew what I wanted to do.

What, for instance?

[From "The Basis of Faith in Art," *The Selected Essays* of
William Carlos Williams. Copyright 1954 by William Carlos
Williams. Reprinted by permission of New Directions Pub-
lishing Corporation.]

I wanted to protest against the blackguardy and beauty of the world, my world.

So you took to poetry.

The only way I could find was poetry—and prose to a lesser extent. So I gradually began to learn, very slowly. If I remember rightly it was more a matter of how I could cling to what I had and not relinquish it in the face of tradition than anything else.

It sounds very simple.

All you have to know is the meaning of the words— and let yourself go.

Then what? What did you learn first?

That it isn't so easy to let yourself go. I had learned too much already, even before I started to write. I ran into good safe stereotype everywhere. Perfectly safe, that's why we cling to it. If I ducked out of that I ran into chaos.

Well?

So I had to begin to invent—or try to invent. Of course I had the advantage of not speaking English. That helped a lot.

And then?

I always knew that I was I, precisely where I stood and that nothing could make me accept anything that had no counterpart in myself by which to recognize it. I always said to myself that I did not speak English, for one thing, and that that should be the basis for a beginning, that I spoke a language that was my own and that I would govern it according to my necessities and not according to unrelated traditions the necessity for whose being had long since passed away. English is full of such compunctions which are wholly irrelevant for a man living as I am today but custom makes it profitable for us to be bound by them. Not me.

*
*
*

A man writes as he does because he doesn't know any better way to do it, to represent exactly what he has to say CLEAN of the destroying, falsifying, besmutching agencies with which he is surrounded. Everything he does is an explanation. He is always trying his very best to refine his work until it is nothing else but "useful knowledge." I say everything, every minutest thing that is part of a work of art is good only when it is useful and that any other explanation of the "work" would be less useful than the work itself.

\*
\*
\*

The difficulty of modern styles is made by the fragmentary stupidity of modern life, its lacunae of sense, loups, perversions of instinct, blankets, amputations, fulsomeness of instruction and multiplications of inanity. To avoid this, accuracy is driven to a hard road. To be plain is to be subverted since every term must be forged new, every word is tricked out of meaning, hanging with as many cheap traps as an altar.

The only human value of anything, writing included, is intense vision of the facts.

# VIRGINIA WOOLF

WE MUST know what we mean when we say that they can write and give us pleasure. We must compare them; we must bring out the quality. We must point to this and say it is good because it is exact, truthful, and imaginative:

Nay, retire men cannot when they would; neither will they, when it were Reason; but are impatient of Privateness, even in age and sickness, which require the shadow: like old Townsmen: that will still be sitting at their street door, though thereby they offer Age to Scorn. . . .

and to this, and say it is bad because it is loose, plausible, and commonplace:

With courteous and precise cynicism on his lips, he thought of quiet virginal chambers, of waters singing under the moon, of terraces where taintless music sobbed into the open night, of pure maternal mistresses with protecting arms and vigilant eyes, of fields slumbering in the sunlight, of leagues of ocean heaving under warm tremulous heavens, of hot ports, gorgeous and perfumed. . . .

It goes on, but already we are bemused with sound and neither feel nor hear. The comparison makes us suspect that the art of writing has for backbone some fierce attachment to an idea. It is on the back of an idea, something believed in with conviction or seen with precision and thus compelling words to its shape, that the diverse company which included Lamb and Bacon, and Mr. Beerbohm and Hudson, and Vernon Lee and Mr. Conrad, and Leslie Stephen and Butler and Walter Pater reaches the farther shore. Very various talents have helped or hindered the passage of the idea into words. Some scrape through painfully; others fly with every wind favouring. But Mr. Belloc and Mr. Lucas and Mr. Lynd and Mr. Squire are not fiercely attached to anything in itself. They share the contemporary dilemma—that lack of an obstinate conviction which lifts ephemeral sounds through the misty sphere of anybody's language to the land where there is a perpetual marriage, a perpetual union. Vague as all definitions are, a good essay must have this permanent quality about it; it must draw its curtain round us, but it must be a curtain that shuts us in, not out.

*
*
*

Literal truth-telling and finding fault with a culprit for his good are out of place in an essay, where everything should be for our good and rather for eternity than for the March number of the *Fortnightly Review*. But if the voice of the scold should never be heard in this narrow plot, there is another voice which is as a plague of locusts—the voice of a man stumbling drowsily among loose words, clutching aimlessly at vague ideas, the voice, for example, of Mr. Hutton in the following passage:

Add to this that his married life was very brief, only seven years and a half, being unexpectedly cut short, and that his passionate reverence for his wife's memory and genius—in his own words, "a religion"—was one which, as he must have been perfectly sensible, he could not make to appear otherwise than extravagant, not to say an hallucination, in the eyes of the rest of mankind, and yet that he was possessed by an irresistible yearning to attempt to embody it in all the tender and enthusiastic hyperbole of which it is so pathetic to find a man who gained his fame by his "dry-light" a master, and it is impossible not to feel that the human incidents in Mr. Mill's career are very sad.

A book could take that blow, but it sinks an essay. A biography in two volumes is indeed the proper depositary; for there, where the licence is so much wider, and hints and glimpses of outside things make part of the feast (we refer to the old type of Victorian volume), these yawns and stretches hardly matter, and have indeed some positive value of their own. But that value, which is contributed by the reader, perhaps illicitly, in his desire to get as much into the book from all possible sources as he can, must be ruled out here.

There is no room for the impurities of literature in an essay. Somehow or other, by dint of labour or bounty of nature, or both combined, the essay must be pure—pure like water or pure like wine, but pure from dullness, deadness, and deposits of extraneous matter.

# Robert Graves
# and Alan Hodge

## FROM *THE READER OVER YOUR SHOULDER*

. . . A question was asked early in 1941 on the employment, in auxiliary Army services, of aliens from the Balkans. It ran:

> In view of the fact that the Bulgarian Government has pursued a course of action very deleterious to this country, ought not applications from Bulgarians to be treated with the greatest reserve?

The questioner was Philip Noel Baker, an acute critic of Government Departments, yet his question was as well-veiled as any Government statement and there were reasons why it should be so. "In view of the fact that" is a purposely loose phrase implying that because the Bulgarians have done $x$ the British Government should do $y$; but it avoids making British action hinge too definitely on Bulgarian action. His Majesty's Government is presumed to be above any small-minded policy of reprisals; it moves independently, keeping the facts large-mindedly "in view," and leaves historians to work out the relationship between them and its course of action—*post hoc* is not necessarily *propter hoc*. "Pursued a course of action"—a course of action and its pursuit suggests a deliberate purposes all kinds of sinister calculations are thus politely imputed to the Bulgarians. "Deleterious" is a euphemism for "bad for us";

[From the previously mentioned work, *The Reader Over Your Shoulder.*]

there may be set-backs, difficulties, obstacles, misfortunes, but it is always presumed that the Government is powerful enough to overcome them. Granted, "deleterious" is originally a very strong word taken over from the Greek ("*deleterios*," destructive), but it has somehow been softened (perhaps by use in advertisements for patent medicines) into meaning "unfavourable in the long run." Finally, "treated with the greatest reserve." This is the official equivalent of "not trusted an inch," and has the advantage of concealing beneath the cloak of diplomatic courtesy the most active forms of distrust: it can mean either taking no notice, or giving the lie direct, or even putting through the third degree. It is almost as useful a covering phrase as "taking the appropriate steps."

. . . So the day-to-day style of a Government Department is full of ambiguous phrases and loosely related clauses—nobody can be quite sure how things will turn out and nobody wishes to commit himself. The following are quotations from more than usually vague minutes (1934-7) circulated in a large Ministry:

While the 80% can be used as a guide, other general conditions must be taken into account, and in particular we should not approve allowances for any particular force much in excess of the allowances at present paid in the generality of forces where circumstances are parallel.

I am rather doubtful whether there·is much to be gained by taking these representations too seriously. On the whole I think the next step, if any, might be to make further enquiries.

This is a border line case, but not, I think, very far over the border: I agree that in this case and in somewhat similar cases an interview at H.O. may save us trouble.

And here is a peremptory reminder from the Stationery Office:

Dear Sir,

I have to call attention to communications from this Department of 3.4.34, 17.4.34 ("refer" and "hastener") and 26.5.34 (letter under above reference) respecting . . . in view of the fact that no reply has yet been received to any of them.

The matter is now urgent to the extent pointed out in the third paragraph of my letter of 26th ultimo.

Yours faithfully

These quotations raise another point: the non-committal timorousness of the official style. A Department does not give away the details of its work: sometimes because they are so complex that no one person fully understands them, sometimes because they are confidential, but more often because of the tradition of anonymous silence observed by the Civil Service in all its contacts with the outside world. Government officials, like members of the British Medical Association, are not allowed to advertise themselves, nor to get into trouble in the newspapers nor to defend themselves if they do. The Minister is briefed to answer for his Department if it is criticized in Parliament and no one else may do so in any other way—except in recent years the Public Relations Officer, who is allowed to write letters to *The Times* in defence of his Department, provided that he does not touch on major matters of policy. One of the effects of this rule is to make officials afraid of publicity. To avoid it they will publish the most indefinite generalities phrased with the most face-saving ingenuity; and when a Department needs to explain something to the public in order to persuade them to some co-operative action, it has to employ professional publicity-men untainted by the habit of official reticence.

*
*
*

As a rule, the best English is written by people without literary pretentions, who have responsible executive jobs in which the use of official language is not compulsory; and, as a rule, the better at their jobs they are, the better they write. Some command a much larger vocabulary than others, are more eloquent and more aware of historic precedent in the use of words; but faults in English prose derive not so much from lack of knowledge, intelligence or art as from lack of thought, patience or goodwill. Though often letters, speeches and reports must be written in a hurry and, because of the countless considerations that clear writing involves, are bound in some way to fall short of the full intended meaning, conscientious people will always regret this necessity and arrange their affairs as far as possible to avoid it. Arnold Bennett in his *Literary Taste* pointed out that faults of style are largely faults of character.

How often has it been said that Carlyle's matter is marred by the harshness and eccentricities of his style? But Carlyle's matter is harsh and eccentric to precisely the same degree as his style. His behaviour was frequently ridiculous, if not abominable.

The writing of good English is thus a moral matter, as the Romans held that the writing of good Latin was.

\*
\*
\*

An unsteady course was followed by English prose through the centuries. Every social and political change was marked by a corresponding change in the character of prose; and it may be assumed that the change in British life which follows the Second World War will be as pronounced as the one that followed the First World War. We hope, but cannot prophesy, that the style of prose best suited to the new conditions will be:

Cleared of encumbrances for quick reading: that is, without unnecessary ornament, irrelevancy, illogicality, ambiguity, repetition, circumlocution, obscurity of reference.

Properly laid out: that is, with each sentence a single step and each paragraph a complete stage in the argument or narrative; with each idea in its right place in the sequence, and none missing; with all connections properly made.

Written in the first place for silent reading, but with consideration for euphony if read aloud.

Consistent in use of language; considerate of the possible limitations of the reader's knowledge; with no indulgence of personal caprice nor any attempt to improve on sincere statement by rhetorical artifice.

Such a style has no chance of immediate adoption in public life, even in contexts where it is realized that officialese is unsuitable and that a simpler, more intimate English must be used.

# SOME PRINCIPLES

*No word or phrase should be ambiguous.*
The most frequent cause of lost battles, political strife, and domestic misunderstanding is ambiguity of terms in reports, orders or requests. Recrimination of the following sort has its parallel at General Head-Quarters after most battles, and at Party Head-Quarters after most lost elections:

Girl: Why didn't you meet me in the break, as I told you?
Boy: You weren't there, darling.
Girl: I was. I waited five minutes.
Boy: That's funny. Didn't you say outside Woolworth's?
Girl: Yes, and you weren't there.
Boy: But I was.
Girl: What? Don't tell me you were fool enough to stand outside Woolworth's when you knew I was getting my toffees at Littlewood's?
Boy: Well, you said Woolworth's. You've just said you said it. Littlewood's isn't Woolworth's.
Girl: It's the same sort of place and you know I always go there for my toffees, stupid. And if you were there, as you say, why didn't you see me as I came out of the Works? I go right past Woolworth's.
Boy: I don't know. Why didn't *you* see *me?* I was there at eleven o'clock sharp.
Girl: Eleven o'clock—no wonder! What a man!
Boy: But you said you'd nip out in your eleven o'clock.
Girl: Oh, you prize-fool! Haven't I told you and told you that in summer-time we have our eleven-o'clock at ten-thirty?

The disastrous charge of the Light Brigade at Balaclava in the Crimean War was made because of a carelessly worded order to 'charge for the guns'—meaning that some British guns which were in an exposed position should be hauled out of reach of the enemy, not that the Russian batteries should be charged. But even in the calmest times it is often very difficult to compose an English sentence that cannot possibly be misunderstood.

## From the Minutes of a Borough Council Meeting:

Councillor Trafford took exception to the proposed notice at the entrance of South Park: 'No dogs must be brought to this Park except on a lead.' He pointed out that this order would not prevent an owner from releasing his pets, or pet, from a lead when once safely inside the park.

*The Chairman* (*Colonel Vine*): What alternative wording would you propose, Councillor?

*Councillor Trafford*: 'Dogs are not allowed in this Park without leads.'

*Councillor Hogg*: Mr. Chairman, I object. The order should be addressed to the owners, not to the dogs.

*Councillor Trafford*: That is a nice point. Very well then: 'Owners of dogs are not allowed in this Park unless they keep them on leads.'

*Councillor Hogg*: Mr. Chairman, I object. Strictly speaking, this would prevent me as a dog-owner from leaving my dog in the back-garden at home and walking with Mrs. Hogg across the Park.

*Councillor Trafford:* Mr. Chairman, I suggest that our legalistic friend be asked to redraft the notice himself.

*Councillor Hogg*: Mr. Chairman, since Councillor Trafford finds it so difficult to improve on my original wording, I accept. 'Nobody without his dog on a lead is allowed in this Park'

*Councillor Trafford*: Mr. Chairman, I object. Strictly speaking, this notice would prevent me, as a citizen who owns no dog, from walking in the Park without first acquiring one.

*Councillor Hogg* (with some warmth): Very simply, then: 'Dogs must be led in this Park.'

*Councillor Trafford*: Mr. Chairman, I object: this reads as if it were a general injunction to the Borough to lead their dogs into the Park.

Councillor Hogg interposed a remark for which he was

called to order; upon his withdrawing it, it was directed to be expunged from the Minutes.

*The Chairman*: Councillor Trafford, Councillor Hogg has had three tries; you have had only two . . .

*Councillor Trafford*: 'All dogs must be kept on leads in this Park.'

*The Chairman*: I see Councillor Hogg rising quite rightly to raise another objection. May I anticipate him with another amendment: 'All dogs in this Park must be kept on the lead.'

This draft was put to the vote and carried unaniomusly, with two abstentions.

From a travel book by Ethel Mannin, 1934:

The Socialist authorities in Vienna built cheap modern flats for the workers.

Were they cheap to build? Or cheap to live in? Or both?

From a despatch to a London newspaper:

An official circular, which fell into the hands of the Polish Government in London, orders the encouragement of improper literature. Dr. Goebbels hopes probably that such literature will help to break morale. It would be rather comic if there were not other methods towards the same goal.

This probably does not mean "If someone told me that this was the only way of breaking Polish morale, I should laugh" but "That is not so comic as it seems at first sight, since the Germans use other, more brutal, means of breaking Polish morale."

In a country village a certain Mrs. Hill wrote to Mrs. Sanders, a neighbour:

Dear Mrs. Sanders:

Will you kindly tell my daughter how much water-glass is a lb, as I bought mine last year and I cannot remember, and I am pickling eggs to-night for the Vicarage? And have you any apples?

Yours
K. Hill

Mrs. Sanders wrote back:

Dear Mrs. Hill:
    A lb of water-glass is about as much as will go into the jam-jar I send you with my little boy. Yes, thank you, I have enough apples to last me through the winter.
Yours,<br>P. SANDERS.

But what Mrs. Hill had meant was: "How much does water-glass cost a pound? I have some left over from last year and don't want to charge the Vicarage an unreasonable price. And may I buy some of your apples?" This is the sort of thing that starts a village feud.

*Every word or phrase should be in its right place in the sentence.*
    Perhaps the most frequently misplaced word in English is "only." In conversation the speaker's accent would make it perfectly plain, for example, what was meant by:

The Council are only warned to do their own repairs.

When written, this may mean either: "The Council are only warned (not instructed) to do their own repairs." or "The Council are given no advice except the warning that they must do their own repairs." But what is meant is perhaps: "The Council are warned to do only their own repairs (not repairs for which they are not legally responsible.)"
    "Either" is another word frequently misplaced. From a written commentary (1941) by Raymond Gram Swing:

The Atlantic, as far as Iceland, either will be left alone by Axis warships, or the United States will be in the shooting war. . . .

It should have been:

Either the Atlantic as far as Iceland will be left alone by Axis warships, or the United States will be in the shooting war. . . .

Here are other miscellaneous examples of misplaced words or phrases.

From a newspaper "short":

Latest reports show that 28,306 children do not go to school in England. More than 4¹/₂ million are getting full-time instruction, 72,505 are receiving part-time schooling.

Far more than 28,306 children do not go to school in England; but in England 28,306 children do not go to school.

*
*
*

*Unless for rhetorical emphasis, or necessary recapitulation, no idea should be presented more than once in the same prose passage.*

Rhetoricians often use a key-word or phrase three times to make it seem holy, important or indisputably true. But, apart from this hoary device, repetitiveness is nowadays considered a sign of pauperdom in oratory, and of feeble-mindedness in narrative.

Undisguised repetition needs no illustration; but here are various examples of concealed repetition. From a published speech by Neville Chamberlain:

We want to see established an international order based upon mutual understanding and mutual confidence, and we cannot build such an order unless it conforms to certain principles which are essential to the establishment of confidence and trust.

When we remove the repeated ideas, this passage reduces to:

The international order that we wish to establish must conform to certain principles of mutual understanding and trust.

From an article by J. Wentworth Day, the agricultural expert:

To-day, the difficulties of defending . . . Greater London have taught us the lesson that to defend the Capital, we must go to the lengths and expense of defence and strategy enough to defend a small country, let alone a great city. . . . That is merely one example of many which I could multiply.

This reduces to:

We have now learned that the defence of Greater London

raises strategic and financial problems that suggest a small country rather than a city. . . . I could quote many such examples.

From a leader (1941) by J. A. Spender:

We are to Russia, as she is to us, one of the imponderables which cannot be weighed in the ordinary diplomatic scales.

This reduces either to:

Russia is to us, as we are to her, an imponderable diplomatic problem.

Or to:

Russia cannot weigh us, nor we her, in the ordinary diplomatic scales.

From "*The Sleeping Beauty* at the London Alhambra," by Sacheverell Sitwell:

. . . But the prospect of five scenes and three hundred dresses by Leon Bakst was in thrilling anticipation for me.

Here, "was in thrilling anticipation for me" should have been merely "thrilled me."

\*
\*
\*

*Sentences and paragraphs should be linked together logically and intelligibly.*

It should always be clear whether a sentence explains, amplifies or limits the statement that it follows; or whether it introduces either a new subject, or a new heading of the original subject.

From a newspaper feature, *All the Year Round in Your Garden*:

Picking over seed-potatoes in the potting shed is a pleasant job. You will find many with ugly blotches and scabs and not be sure whether they will favour your prospects of a good crop. . . .

The connection between these two sentences is blurred.

Either the second should begin a new paragraph, to show that the gardener's anxieties about his crop do not illustrate the pleasantness of the job; or else it should be introduced with a "But."

From memoirs published in a provincial paper:

On leaving the hospital of Saint Antoine, I remember, the Empress Eugénie was carried almost to her carriage by the crowd, who eagerly pressed around her, weeping, kissing her hands and heaping blessings on her head. But the most comical event of the day was when a coal-black negro from Dahomey presented himself at the Palace with a basket of freshly caught fish. . . .

Here the "But" is illogical, because it suggests that the simple enthusiasm of the crowd was also comical.

From a book-review by Basil de Sélincourt:

Having loved Ruskin unsubdued, he [Sydney Cockerell] was ready to love and be loved by everybody; as the girl friend who later became a nun wrote to him from her novice cell: "You do seem to have a remarkable capacity for meeting distinguished people." That is it; they are all here; Hardy, Doughty, Lawrence, Blunt, Mrs. Hardy, Lady Burne-Jones, Charlotte Mew. . . .

The phrase "as the girl friend wrote" purports to justify the statement that Sydney Cockerell was ready to love and be loved by *everyone;* but all that it provides is a (possibly ironical) reference to his being ready to love and be loved by distinguished people.

Here is part of an article by Admiral C. J. Eyrès:

The Germans in the last war, in the use of lethal gas and unrestricted submarine warfare, acted disgracefully and immorally, just because the German Government had formally, by Treaty, denounced their use, and were dishonouring their bond.

The "just because" should be "for" or "since". Either of these words would explain why the Admiral considered the

Germans to have acted "disgracefully and immorally." The "because" suggests that the motive for the Germans' disgraceful and immoral actions was merely to flout a previous renunciation by their Government of the use of certain weapons. (He probably means "renounced," not "denounced.")

From an address to the University of Oxford by Viscount Halifax, its Chancellor:

> What has, for example, been the driving force behind the Nazi movement in Germany? It has been German youth. . . . Their point of view stands in stark opposition to yours. They do not understand your way of thinking. Your ideals mean nothing to them. . . .
> The real conflict, therefore, to-day is not between age and youth, but between youth and youth. . . .

The "therefore" is illogical, unless Lord Halifax is washing his hands of the conflict on the ground that it is not of his making.

*
*
*

> *The order of ideas in a sentence or paragraph should such that the reader need not rearrange them in his mind.*

The natural arrangement of ideas in critical argument is:

Statement of problem.

Marshalling of evidence, first on main points, then on subsidiary ones—the same sequence kept throughout the argument.

Credibility of evidence examined.

Statement of possible implications of all evidence not wholly rejected.

The weighing of conflicting evidence in the scale of probability.

Verdict.

The natural arrangement of ideas in historical writing is the one recommended in *Alice in Wonderland* by the King of Hearts to the White Rabbit:

Begin at the beginning, and go on till you come to the end: then stop.

. . . It would take up too much space to analyse a mishandled argument in full. But readers will be familiar with the sort of argument that, if it ever commits itself to a statement of the problem, does not do so until a mass of jumbled evidence on subsidiary points has been adduced, after which it gives the verdict, and then evidence on the principal point, and then an irrelevant report on "what the soldier's wife said", and then contradictory statements about evidence on subsidiary points, and then perhaps a reconsideration of the verdict, and then fresh evidence, and finally a restatement of the verdict. Doubts are cast by modern mathematicians on the universal validity of the conclusions reached by Euclid in his propositions; but at least he knew how to handle an argument, and always wound up with "This conclusion should be tested by practical experiment".

We shall, however, quote part of a carelessly constructed argument by Major-Gen. Sir Andrew McCulloch. It is from his answer to an editorial question (October 1941): "Do you think that any form of British invasion of Europe would be possible during the next weeks or months?"

I think it feasible to force an entry into Europe. This opinion, however, is of little value, because I do not know what force is available. If I knew as much as Mr. Churchill or the Chiefs of Staff my views might be of value. As it is, my opinions are in the realm of dreams. For this reason I shall take a purely imaginative situation, and on this premiss shall discuss the relative merits of landing at various places on the coast of Europe.

The logical order of ideas in this passage is:

1 If I knew as well as Mr. Churchill or the Chiefs
of Staff

2 what forces are available

3 my views might be of value

4 but I do not know,

5 and, when, therefore,

6 after discussing the comparative merits of various
landing-places,

7 I pronounce it feasible to force an entry into Europe,

8 my premisses

9 must be recognized as no less imaginative

10 than if I had dreamed them.

The order in the original is 7, 4, 2, 1, 3, 10, 5, 9, 8, 6.

\*
\*
\*

*Metaphors should not be mated in such a way as to
confuse or distract the reader.*

Metaphors are used more often in English than in most
modern European languages, and far more often than in
Latin or Greek. A metaphor is a condensed simile. Here
are two similes:

Marriage is like a lottery—with a great many blanks and
very few prizes.

Our struggle against sin resembles a cricket-match. Just as
the batsman strides out to the wicket, armed with pads, gloves
and bat, and manfully stands up to demon bowling, with an
adversary behind him always ready to stump him or catch him
out . . . and when the sun sets, and stumps are drawn, he
modestly carries his bat back to the pavilion, amid plaudits. So
likewise the Christian . . . And when, finally, safe in the celestial
pavilion, he lays aside the bat of the spirit, unbuckles the pads
of faith, removes the gloves of doctrine and casts down the cap
of sanctity upon the scoring-table,—lo, inside, is the name of
The Maker!

Examples of metaphors derived from these two similes are:

Poor Edwin has indeed drawn a blank in the matrimonial
lottery.

St. Paul, that great sportsman, faced the bowling manfully in the struggle against Paganism.

When two unconnected similes are reduced to metaphors, and these are combined in the same sentence, the effect on the reader is to blur both of the mental pictures which the metaphors call up:

Edwin's matrimonial record deserves our praise rather than our pity: he drew two blanks but on each occasion faced the bowling manfully.

The mismating of metaphors is justified only in facetious contexts. For example, Mr. R. A. Butler, M.P., remarked in a Commons debate:

The Hon. Member for East Wolverhampton is to be congratulated on producing a very tasty rehash of several questions which have been fully ventilated in this House up to date.

Here, the unpleasant implications of the word "ventilated" were sure of a laugh. The columnist "Atticus" often makes genial use of the mismated metaphor. For example:

Colonel Moore-Brabazon's predecessor, Sir John Reith, continues on his Gulliver's travels, and is now on his way to that distant land, the House of Lords, from whose bourne no traveller returns.

But there is no facetiousness in this remark by Mr. Arthur Greenwood, M.P. (1939):

While we strive for peace, we are leaving no stone unturned to meet the situation should the fateful blow fall.

In what conceivable circumstances could anyone turn up a stone to ward off a fateful blow? Mr. Greenwood meant:

We who strive for peace are seeking every means of warding off the fateful blow.

\*
\*
\*

*Except where the writer is being deliberately facetious, all phrases in a sentence, or sentences in a paragraph, should belong to the same vocabulary or level of language.*

Scholars and clergymen are seldom able to keep their language all of a piece.

The following is from a newspaper sermon:

It is one of the mysteries of that inner life of man (one so replete with mysteries hard to accept or solve) that some of us are clearly, as it were, freeborn citizens of grace, whilst others—alas! many others—can only at great price buy this freedom. Of this there can be no doubt. The Gospel appointed for to-day reports to us, in the words of our Lord Himself, a story at once simple and mystifying, about day-labourers in an Eastern vineyard. Some of them had worked a full day, whilst others had only "clocked in", so to speak, when it was nearly time to go. Yet each received from the employer the same flat rate of remuneration—a Roman penny. Our Lord said that was all right, which must be enough for us.

It begins with ecclesiastical-scholarly language "whilst others—alas! many others—can only at great price buy this freedom"; gradually presses through the apologetically modern, "others had only 'clocked in', so to speak, when it was nearly time to go", and the commercial, "each received from the employer the same flat rate of remuneration"; descends to the downright vulgar, "Our Lord said that was all right. . . ."

\*
\*
\*

*Sentences should not be so long that the reader loses his way in them.*

A sentence may be as long as the writer pleases, provided that he confines it to a single connected range of ideas, and by careful punctuation prevents the reader from finding it either tedious or confusing. Modern journalists work on the principle that sentences should be as snappy as possible; they seldom, therefore, use colons or semicolons. Historians and biographers have learned to be snappy too. Here is H. C. Armstrong writing about Mustapha Kemal Ataturk in his *Grey Wolf*:

> Enver was always inspired by great ideas, by far-flung schemes. The big idea absorbed him. He cared nothing for details, facts or figures.

Sentences by eighteenth-century authors sometimes continue for a page or more, yet are not allowed to get out of hand. Here, however, are a couple of modern instances where even a seven-line sentence is too long.

From an article by D. R. Gent, the sporting-journalist:

> I spent many hours dipping into Rugby books of all kinds, and two especially suggested lots of subjects that, I think, will interest my readers these days, when we can face up to the strenuous times we are living in, even more bravely when we can refresh ourselves occasionally with memories of great days behind us, and especially days on the Rugby field or watching glorious matches.

This would have read better if he had broken it up into three sentences, in some such way as this:

> I spent many hours dipping into a variety of books about Rugby and two especially interested me. I think that they would have interested my readers too, for they concerned great events in the history of the game. In these strenuous times we can face up to our trials and responsibilities more bravely if we occasionally refresh ourselves with memories of the glorious matches which we have witnessed or in which we have been fortunate enough to take part ourselves.

This is from an article by Ernest Newman, the music critic:

> Berlioz's faults as a composer are obvious, but not more so than those of many other composers who, however, had the good luck to have their misses counted as hits by umpires whose sense of values had been perverted by too long a toleration of bad art so long as it was bad in the orthodox way, whereas Berlioz's directest hits were often debited to him as misses.

This is too long a sentence only because it is mismanaged. Commas are not enough to separate so many complex ideas into properly related parts of a single argument. We suggest this alternative version:

> Berlioz's faults are obvious to us modern listeners, as are those of many other composers who in their time fared far better with the critics than he did: their misses were often counted as hits, his most direct hits as misses—merely because musical standards had been perverted by a long toleration of work which, though bad, was not eccentrically so.

# *Interludes*

# 2

Robert Frost makes a characteristic connection between the style and the man, and Viriginia Woolf
has some further thoughts on language as the expression of character or personality. Hemingway
briefly, and Pound at greater length, defend the
integrity and importance of good prose.

# ROBERT FROST

A dramatic necessity goes deep into the nature of the sentence. Sentences are not different enough to hold the attention unless they are dramatic. No ingenuity of varying structure will do. All that can save them is the speaking tone of voice somehow entangled in the words and fastened to the page for the ear of the imagination. That is all that can save poetry from sing-song, all that can save prose from itself.

*<br>*<br>*

The style is the man. Rather say the style is the way the man takes himself; and to be at all charming or even bearable, the way is almost rigidly prescribed. If it is with outer seriousness, it must be with inner humor. If it is with outer humor, it must be with inner seriousness. Neither one alone without the other under it will do. Robinson was thinking as much in his sonnet on Tom Hood. One ordeal of Mark Twain was the constant fear that his occluded seriousness would be overlooked. That betrayed him into his two or three books of out-and-out seriousness.

[From the Preface to *A Way Out* from *Selected Prose of Robert Frost*, edited by Hyde Cox and Edward Connery Lathem. Copyright © 1966 by Holt, Rinehart & Winston, Inc. Reprinted by permission of Holt, Rinehart & Winston, Inc. The second selection is from the Introduction to *King Jasper* by Edward Arlington Robinson. Reprinted with permission of The Macmillan Company. Copyright 1935 by The Macmillan Company, renewed 1963 by The Macmillan Company.]

# VIRGINIA WOOLF

. . . Once again we have an essayist capable of using the essayist's most proper but most dangerous and delicate tool. He has brought personality into literature, not unconsciously and impurely, but so consciously and purely that we do not know whether there is any relation between Max the essayist and Mr. Beerbohm the man. We only know that the spirit of personality permeates every word that he writes. The triumph is the triumph of style. For it is only by knowing how to write that you can make use in literature of your self; that self which, while it is essential to literature, is also its most dangerous antagonist. Never to be yourself and yet always—that is the problem. Some of the essayists in Mr. Rhys' collection, to be frank, have not altogether succeeded in solving it. We are nauseated by the sight of trivial personalities decomposing in the eternity of print. As talk, no doubt, it was charming, and certainly the writer is a good fellow to meet over a bottle of beer. But literature is stern; it is no use being charming, virtuous, or even learned and brilliant into the bargain, unless, she seems to reiterate, you fulfil her first condition—to know how to write.

\*
\*
\*

. . . If the essay admits more properly than biography or fiction of sudden boldness and metaphor, and can be polished till every atom of its surface shines, there are dangers in that too. We are soon in sight of ornament. Soon the current, which is the life-blood of literature, runs slow; and instead of sparkling and flashing or moving with a quieter impulse which has a deeper excitement, words coagulate together in frozen sprays which, like the grapes on a Christmas-tree, glitter for a single night, but are dusty and garish the day after. The temptation to decorate is great where the theme may be of the slightest.

[From the previously mentioned collection of essays, *The Common Reader*.]

# ERNEST HEMINGWAY

. . . No matter how good a phrase or a simile he may have if he puts it in where it is not absolutely necessary and irreplaceable he is spoiling his work for egotism. Prose is architecture, not interior decoration, and the Baroque is over.

[This selection from Hemingway is also from *Death in the Afternoon*.]

# EZRA POUND

IT IS very difficult to make people understand the *impersonal* indignation that a decay of writing can cause men who understand what it implies, and the end whereto it leads. It is almost impossible to express any degree of such indignation without being called "embittered", or something of that sort.

Nevertheless the "statesman cannot govern, the scientist cannot participate his discoveries, men cannot agree on wise action without language", and all their deeds and conditions are affected by the defects or virtues of idiom.

A people that grows accustomed to sloppy writing is a people in process of losing grip on its empire and on itself. And this looseness and blowsiness is not anything as simple and scandalous as abrupt and disordered syntax.

It concerns the relation of expression to meaning. Abrupt and disordered syntax can be at times very honest, and an elaborately constructed sentence can be at times merely an elaborate camouflage.

\*
\*
\*

Literature does not exist in a vacuum. Writers as such have a definite social function exactly proportioned to their ability AS WRITERS. This is their main use. All other

[These selections are from the previously mentioned work, *The ABC of Reading* and from *The Literary Essays* of Ezra Pound. All rights reserved. Reprinted by permission of New Directions Publishing Corporation and Faber & Faber Ltd.]

uses are relative, and temporary, and can be estimated only in relation to the views of a particular estimator.

Partisans of particular ideas may value writers who agree with them more than writers who do not, they may, and often do, value bad writers of their own party or religion more than good writers of another party or church.

But there is one basis susceptible of estimation and independent of all questions of viewpoint.

Good writers are those who keep the language efficient. That is to say, keep it accurate, keep it clear. It doesn't matter whether the good writer wants to be useful, or whether the bad writer wants to do harm.

Language is the main means of human communication. If an animal's nervous system does not transmit sensations and stimuli, the animal atrophies.

If a nation's literature declines, the nation atrophies and decays.

Your legislator can't legislate for the public good, your commander can't command, your populace (if you be a democratic country) can't instruct its "representatives", save by language.

The fogged language of swindling classes serves only a temporary purpose.

A limited amount of communication *in re* special subjects, passes via mathematical formulae, via the plastic arts, via diagrams, via purely musical forms, but no one proposes substituting these for the common speech, nor does anyone suggest that it would be either possible or advisable.

## *Ubicunque Lingua Romana, Ibi Roma*[1]

Greece and Rome civilized BY LANGUAGE. Your language is in the care of your writers.

['Insults o'er dull and speechless tribes']

1. Wherever the Roman language is, is Rome.

but this language is not merely for records of great things done. Horace and Shakespeare can proclaim its monumental and mnemonic value, but that doesn't exhaust the matter.

Rome rose with the idiom of Caesar, Ovid, and Tacitus, she declined in a welter of rhetoric, the diplomat's "language to conceal thought", and so forth.

The man of understanding can no more sit quiet and resigned while his country lets its literature decay, and lets good writing meet with contempt, than a good doctor could sit quiet and contented while some ignorant child was infecting itself with tuberculosis under the impression that it was merely eating jam tarts.

*<br/>*<br/>*

. . . Has literature a function in the state, in the aggregation of humans, in the republic, in *res publica*, which ought to mean the public convenience (despite the slime of bureaucracy, and the execrable taste of the populace in selecting its rulers)? It has.

And this function is *not* the coercing or emotionally persuading, or bullying or suppressing people into the acceptance of any one set or any six sets of opinions as opposed to any other one set or half-dozen sets of opinions.

It has to do with the clarity and vigour of "any and every" thought and opinion. It has to do with maintaining the very cleanliness of the tools, the health of the very matter of thought itself. Save in the rare and limited instances of invention in the plastic arts, or in mathematics, the individual cannot think and communicate his thought, the governor and legislator cannot act effectively or frame his laws, without words, and the solidity and validity of these words is in the care of the damned and despised *litterati*. When their work goes rotten—by that I do not mean when they express indecorous thoughts—but when their very medium, the very essence of their work, the application of word to thing goes rotten, i.e. becomes slushy and inexact, or excessive or bloated, the whole machinery of social and of individual thought and order goes to pot. This is a lesson of history, and a lesson not yet halflearned.

The great writers need no debunking.

The pap is not in them, and doesn't need to be squeezed out. They do not lend themselves to imperial and sentimental exploitations. A civilization was founded on Homer, civilization not a mere bloated empire. The Macedonian domination rose and grew after the sophists. It also subsided.

It is not only a question of rhetoric, of loose expression, but also of the loose use of individual words. What the renaissance gained in direct examination of natural phenomena, it in part lost in losing the feel and desire for exact descriptive terms. I mean that the medieval mind had little but words to deal with, and it was more careful in its definitions and verbiage. It did not define a gun in terms that would just as well define an explosion, nor explosions in terms that would define triggers.

Misquoting Confucius, one might say: It does not matter whether the author desire the good of the race or acts merely from personal vanity. The thing is mechanical in action. In proportion as his work is exact, i.e., true to human consciousness and to the nature of man, as it is exact in formulation of desire, so is it durable and so is it "useful"; I mean it maintains the precision and clarity of thought, not merely for the benefit of a few dilettantes and "lovers of literature", but maintains the health of thought outside literary circles and in non-literary existence, in general individual and communal life.

Or *dans ce genre on n'émeut que par la clarté.* One moves the reader only by clarity. In depicting the motions of the "human heart" the durability of the writing depends on the exactitude. It is the thing that is true and stays true that keeps fresh for the new reader.

*
*
*

In Europe, if you ask a man to define anything, his definition always moves away from the simple things that he knows perfectly well, it recedes into an unknown region, that is a region of remoter and progressively remoter abstraction.

Thus if you ask him what red is, he says it is a "colour."

If you ask him what a colour is, he tells you it is a vibration or a refraction of light, or a division of the spectrum.

And if you ask him what vibration is, he tells you it is a mode of energy, or something of that sort, until you arrive at a modality of being, or non-being, or at any rate you get in beyond your depth, and beyond his depth.

In the middle ages when there wasn't any material science, as we now understand it, when human knowledge could not make automobiles run, or electricity carry language through the air, etc., etc., in short, when learning consisted in little more than splitting up of terminology, there was a good deal of care for terminology, and the general exactitude in the use of abstract terms may have been (probably was) higher.

I mean a mediaeval theologian took care not to define a dog in terms that would have applied just as well to a dog's tooth or its hide, or the noise it makes when lapping water; but all your teachers will tell you that science developed more rapidly after Bacon had suggested the direct examination of phenomena, and after Galileo and others had stopped discussing things so much, and had begun really to look at them, and to invent means (like the telescope) of seeing them better.

\*
\*
\*

Roughly then, Good writing is writing that is perfectly controlled, the writer says just what he means. He says it with complete clarity and simplicity. He uses the smallest possible number of words. I do not mean that he skimps paper, or that he screws about like Tacitus to get his thought crowded into the least possible space. But, granting that two sentences are at times easier to understand than one sentence containing the double meaning, the author tries to communicate with the reader with the greatest possible despatch, save where for any one of forty reasons he does not wish to do so.

Also there are various kinds of clarity. There is the clarity of the request: Send me four pounds of ten-penny nails. And there is the syntactical simplicity of the requests: Buy me the kind of Rembrandt I like. This last is an utter cryptogram. It presupposes a more complex and intimate understanding of the speaker than most of us ever acquire of anyone. It has as many meanings, almost, as there are persons who might speak it. To a stranger it conveys nothing at all.

It is the almost constant labour of the prose artist to translate this latter kind of clarity into the former; to say "Send me the kind of Rembrandt I like" in the terms of "Send me four pounds of ten-penny nails."

The whole thing is an evolution. In the beginning simple words were enough: Food; water; fire. Both prose and poetry are but an extension of language. Man desires to communicate with his fellows. He desires an ever increasingly complicated communication. Gesture serves up to a point. Symbols may serve. When you desire something not present to the eye or when you desire to communicate ideas, you must have recourse to speech. Gradually you wish to communicate something less bare and ambiguous than ideas. You wish to communicate an idea and its modifications, an idea and a crowd of its effects, atmospheres, contradictions. You wish to question whether a certain formula works in every case, or in what per cent of cases, etc., etc., etc., you get the Henry James novel.

You wish to communicate an idea and its concomitant emotions, or an emotion and its concomitant ideas, or a sensation and its derivative emotions, or an impression that is emotive, etc., etc., etc. You begin with the yeowl and the bark, and you develop into the dance and into music, and into music with words, and finally into words with music, and finally into words with a vague adumbration of music, words suggestive of music, words measured, or words in a rhythm that preserves some accurate trait of the emotive impression, or of the sheer character of the fostering or parental emotion.

When this rhythm, or when the vowel and consonantal melody or sequence seems truly to bear the trace of emotion which the poem (for we have come at last to the poem) is intended to communicate, we say that this part of the work is good. And "this part of the work" is by now "technique". That "dry, dull, pedantic" technique, that all bad artists rail against. It is only a part of technique, it is rhythm, cadence, and the arrangement of sounds.

Also the "prose", the words and their sense must be such as fit the emotion. Or, from the other side, ideas, or fragments of ideas, the emotion and concomitant emotions of this "Intellectual and Emotional Complex" (for we have come to the intellectual and emotional complex) must be in harmony, they must form an organism, they must be an oak sprung from an acorn.

# Edmund Wilson

## MR. JOSEPH E. DAVIES AS A STYLIST

I have just been reading *Mission to Moscow*, Mr. Joseph
E. Davies' book, after seeing the film of the same title. The
picture, I find, coincides with the book in almost no respect. The real Mr. Joseph Davies, for example, is a shrewd
corporation lawyer who contributed to the Roosevelt campaign fund and was appropriately rewarded with an ambas-
sadorship. The Davies of the Warner Brothers picture is
a plain rugged American business man, played by Mr.
Walter Huston rather like a more elderly version of Sinclair Lewis's Dodsworth, who demurs with a touching
humility when the President asks him to go to Russia, and
protests that he is really not qualified because he has had
no diplomatic training. The real Mr. Davies was sent for
the perfectly specific purpose of discussing a trade agreement and arranging for the settlement of debts contracted
by the Kerensky government. But these objectives do not
figure in the film. The Hollywood Mr. Davies is simply
entrusted with a mission of reporting on the Soviet Union.
The real Mr. Davies was troubled by the tyrannies of the
Stalinist police state. "No physical betterment of living
standards," he wrote in *Mission to Moscow*, "could possibly compensate for the utter destruction of liberty of
thought or speech and the sanctity of the individual. . . .
The government is a dictatorship not 'of the proletariat,'
as professed, but 'over the proletariat.' It is completely

[From the collection *Classics and Commercials*. Reprinted
by permission of the author.]

dominated by one man." One could quote him in this sense at length.

There is one point, however, in which the film is quite faithful to the real Mr. Davies. When the Davies of Walter Huston is made to attend the Moscow trials, he enunciates the following statement: "Based on twenty years of trial practice, I'd be inclined to believe these men's testimony." The trials themselves, it is true, are represented falsely, and this is not precisely the kind of thing that Mr. Davies was saying about them at the time; but the undependable syntax of the Warner Brothers' Davies is absolutely true to life. I should say, indeed, from reading the book, that the author of *Mission to Moscow* is, so far as my knowledge extends, the greatest master of bad official English since the late President Harding.

The prose style of President Harding has been analyzed by H. L. Mencken in his admirable little paper, *A Short View of Gamalielese;* and this piece, which I have lately been rereading, has stimulated me to try to do some justice to the beauties of Mr. Davies' writing.

Let me begin with one of the cultural notes with which Davies the connoisseur and man of taste diversifies his record of affairs of state, a passage which illustrates brilliantly his skill in producing the effect of surprise:

> For weeks there have been celebrations of the centenary of Pushkin's death all over the country. He is a combination of Byron and Shakespeare for the Russian people. He was a liberal in thought and married to a noblewoman who, it is alleged, was a mistress of the tsar. He was killed in a duel, which, as the story goes, was a frame-up. Both the opera and the ballet were based on Pushkin's works and the music was by the great Tchaikovsky. The opera was *Eugen Onegin,* a romantic story of two young men of position whose friendship was broken up over a misunderstanding and lovers' quarrel which resulted in a duel in which the poet was killed. It was significant of Pushkin's own end and oddly enough was written by him.

The sequence of relative pronouns here in the sentence before the last, each one depending on the one before, is a very fine bit of writing, but it only prepares for the climax. It drags us, by a series of hitches, up an incline like the hump on a roller-coaster, from the top of which we suddenly dip into a dizzying and breath-depriving excitement. What is it that makes the next sentence so startling? Not syntax, for the syntax is normal. Not logic: no mere fallacy is involved. We cannot assign this sleight to any of the familiar categories of rhetorical or logical error. The device is original and daring; it takes us a moment to grasp it; but then we become aware that the trick consists of first explaining that the opera which Mr. Davies calls *Eugen Onegin* (though this is neither the Russian nor the English form of the title) is based on Pushkin's poem; then of indicating a striking parallel between the circumstances of Pushkin's death and the poem; and then of suddenly making the point that, by some scarcely believable coincidence, the poem was written by Pushkin. But to paraphrase the passage thus is to rob it of all its thrill. The whole effect depends on the quickness of the shift in the sense and on the simple phrase *oddly enough*, at once arresting and casual. Only a bad writer of special gifts could have hit upon and placed this phrase. It is as if a long red carpet upon which we had been walking, on our way to some ceremony of state, had suddenly been pulled out from under us.

There is, however, one example even bolder of Mr. Davies' ability to baffle and to dazzle:

> The peace of Europe, if maintained, is in imminent danger of being a peace imposed by the dictators, under conditions where all of the smaller countries will speedily rush in to get under the shield of the German aegis, and under conditions where, even though there be a concert of power, as I have predicted to you two years ago, with "Hitler leading the band."

Here the opening is weighty and portentous: a veteran man of affairs with a large experience of Europe is about to deliver a considered opinion. The first indication of anything queer comes with *the shield of the German aegis;*

but although this gives us pause for a moment, we immediately reassure ourselves by concluding that Mr. Davies surely knows that a shield is an aegis, and has allowed himself the little tautology, in the exuberance of his enjoyment of his official position, as a mere rhetorical flourish. But then we come to the *as I have predicted to you two years ago.* The tense here is incorrect: it should be *as I predicted to you two years ago.* We conclude that Mr. Davies does not know this, but that, even though he does not know it, the instinct of his genius has guided him to hit upon the perfect deviation which, by adding to the solemnity of the tone at the same time as to the absurdity of the writing, will lead the way to the final effect. And what an effect it is! The sentence never comes to a conclusion. It is a new sort of aposiopesis—an aposiopesis with a full-stop at the end. Yet the grammatical impossibility has with wonderful art been half-concealed. The writer has first given us an adverbial clause beginning with *under conditions where,* which completes itself in the logical way, but then he has gone on to another clause, which begins in the same way: *and under conditions where.* Since we have just seen the first one brought off, we are prepared for the fulfilment of the second. But this second clause is never completed. Mr. Davies, by a rare stroke of art, starts another subordinate clause, *even though there be,* etc., and at the end of this clause he stops. On first reading, we fail to grasp it; we go back and read the sentence again. The use of the subjunctive here, *even though there be,* is another of his fine manipulations to give us confidence in the structure of his thought. We find it very hard to believe that a man who can use the subjunctive in this noble traditional way would be capable of leaving his sentence with one end sticking out in the air, like the rope in the Indian rope trick. And yet Mr. Davies *has* left it so, and we can only accept and wonder, just as we can only accept and wonder at his giving the public his word for the authenticity of all the testimony that is supposed to be quoted, in his film, from the records of the Moscow trials and that includes a confession by Tukhachevsky imagined and written by Hollywood; at his flying back from Moscow on his second mission with the advertisement *Mission to Moscow* painted, in English and Russian, in large yellow letters on his plane; and at his watching with gratification, in the company of Stalin and his retinue, while this film was shown in the Kremlin.

Let me finally quote a passage less distinguished by brilliance of language than by the felicity with which it mirrors the qualities of the man himself. Mr. Davies is reporting an interview with a representative of the Soviet Foreign Office, at which the trade agreement and the debts were discussed:

> He stated that they were having difficulty, in connection with guaranteeing $4,000,000 of purchases in the United States. . . . I stated quite frankly, however, that while, personally, I made these admissions to him "and against interest," that [*sic*] quite frankly I had absolutely no tolerance for a position that would haggle over an increase of $10,000,000 in purchases (from $30,000,000 to $40,000,000) in view of both the equities and the practicalities of this situation; that in my opinion it was not an evidence of approaching the matter in a broad-minded and appreciative attitude of the position which Secretary Hull had taken so fairly and in such a large-minded way on this particular problem.

The style here, of course, is remarkable, as Mr. Davies' style always is. The superfluous *that* is good. The *broad-minded* and *large-minded* are like the flourish of persuasive hands brushing doubts and inhibitions aside; and in the next sentence but one we already see the spell that is cast by the verbal incantation, taking effect on the Soviet department head:

> Mr. Neymann manifested a very fair-minded attitude in reply and stated in conclusion that he would not be disposed to quarrel with that point of view. . . .

But there glints through in this passage, when the figures are named, the relentless *fortiter in rebus*—to re-

sort to a kind of ornament much relished by Mr. Davies—
which always lurks behind his *sauviter in modo.* Mr.
Davies is of Welsh blood, he tells us, and, like a Welsh-
man, he knows how to combine an elevated and shim-
mering eloquence with a certain subtlety of practical
shrewdness. The glint is half lost in the mist; the purpose
is half obscured by the shower of flattering words that,
meaningless though most of them are, rather soothe us
and please us as we read. These words may perhaps have
made it easier for Mr. Davies, at the time of his embassy,
to further the interests of the United States; but there
are moments when the metallic gleam that pierces from
time to time the shifting lights of Mr. Davies' language,
has the look of an eye fixed intently on opportunities for
conspicuous self-dramatization.

# *Interludes*

# 3

Pound continues to demonstrate that style is a moral matter. Quiller-Couch makes his point more lightly by a translation of Hamlet's soliloquy into bad modern prose. Thurber's anecdotes about his old editor provide a model for the writer who is editing his own work.

# EZRA POUND

THIS brings us to the immorality of bad art. Bad art is inaccurate art. It is art that makes false reports. If a scientist falsifies a report either deliberately or through negligence we consider him as either a criminal or a bad scientist according to the enormity of his offence, and he is punished or despised accordingly.

*<br>*<br>*

One does not need to read black print to learn this ethical fact about physicians. Yet it takes a deal of talking to convince a layman that bad art is "immoral". And that good art however "immoral" it is, is wholly a thing of virtue. Purely and simply that good art can NOT be immoral. By good art I mean art that bears true witness, I mean the art that is most precise. You can be wholly precise in representing a vagueness. You can be wholly a liar in pretending that the particular vagueness was precise in its outline. If you cannot understand this with regard to poetry, consider the matter in terms of painting.

*<br>*<br>*

It is as important for the purpose of thought to keep language efficient as it is in surgery to keep tetanus bacilli out of one's bandages.

In introducing a person to literature one would do well to have him examine works where language is efficiently used; to devise a system for getting directly and expeditiously at such works, despite the smokescreens erected by half-knowing and half-thinking critics. To get at them, despite the mass of dead matter that these people have heaped up and conserved round about them in the proportion: one barrel of sawdust to each half-bunch of grapes.

[Selections from the previously mentioned work, *The Literary Essays* of Ezra Pound.]

Great literature is simply language charged with meaning to the ultmost possible degree.

# SIR ARTHUR QUILLER-COUCH

A lesson about writing your language may go deeper than language; for language . . . is your reason. . . . So long as you prefer abstract words, which express other men's summarised concepts of things, to concrete ones which lie as near as can be reached to things themselves and are the first-hand material for your thoughts, you will remain, at the best, writers at second-hand. If your language be jargon, your intellect, if not your whole character, will almost certainly correspond. Where your mind should go straight, it will dodge: the difficulties it should approach with a fair front and grip with a firm hand it will be seeking to evade or circumvent. For the style is the man, and where a man's treasure is there his heart, and his brain, and his writing, will be also.

\*
\*
\*

To begin with, let me plead that you have been told of one or two things which Style is *not;* which have little or nothing to do with Style, though sometimes vulgarly mistaken for it. Style, for example, is not—can never be— extraneous Ornament. You remember, may be, the Persian lover whom I quoted to you out of Newman: how to convey his passion he sought a professional letter-writer and purchased a vocabulary charged with ornament, wherewith to attract the fair one as with a basket of jewels. Well, in this extraneous, professional, purchased ornamentation, you have something which Style *is not:* and if you here require a practical rule of me, I will present you with this: "Whenever you feel an impulse to perpetrate a piece of exceptionally fine writing, obey it—whole-heartedly—and

[From Sir Arthur Quiller-Couch, *On the Art of Writing.* Reprinted by permission of the Cambridge University Press, Copyright 1923.]

delete it before sending your manuscript to press. *Murder your darlings.*"

\*
\*
\*

. . . Let us . . . attempt to illustrate jargon by the converse method of taking a famous piece of English (say Hamlet's soliloquy) and remoulding a few lines of it in this fashion:—

To be, or the contrary? Whether the former or the latter be preferable would seem to admit of some difference of opinion; the answer in the present case being of an affirmative or of a negative character according as to whether one elects on the one hand to mentally suffer the disfavour of fortune, albeit in an extreme degree, or on the other to boldly envisage adverse conditions in the prospect of eventually bringing them to a conclusion. The condition of sleep is similar to, if not indistinguishable from that of death; and with the addition of finality the former might be considered identical with the latter: so that in this connection it might be argued with regard to sleep that, could the addition be effected, a termination would be put to the endurance of a multiplicity of inconveniences, not to mention a number of down-right evils incidental to our fallen humanity, and thus a consummation achieved of a most gratifying nature.

That is jargon: and to write jargon is to be perpetually shuffling around in the fog and cotton-wool of abstract terms; to be for ever hearkening, like Ibsen's Peer Gynt, to the voice of the Boyg exhorting you to circumvent the difficulty, to beat the air because it is easier than to flesh your sword in the thing. The first virtue, the touchstone of masculine style, is its use of the active verb and the concrete noun. When you write in the active voice, "They gave him a silver teapot," you write as a man. When you write "He was made the recipient of a silver teapot," you write jargon.

# JAMES THURBER

HAVING a manuscript under Ross's scrutiny was like putting your car in the hands of a skilled mechanic, not an automotive engineer with a bachelor of science degree, but a guy who knows what makes a motor go, and sputter, and wheeze, and sometimes come to a dead stop; a man with an ear for the faintest body squeak as well as the loudest engine rattle. When you first gazed, appalled, upon an uncorrected proof of one of your stories or articles, each margin had a thicket of queries and complaints—one writer got a hundred and forty-four on one profile. It was as though you beheld the works of your car spread all over the garage floor, and the job of getting the thing together again and making it work seemed impossible. Then you realized that Ross was trying to make your Model T or old Stutz Bearcat into a Cadillac or Rolls-Royce. He was at work with the tools of his unflagging perfectionism, and, after an exchange of growls or snarls, you set to work to join him in his enterprise.

Ross's marginal questions and comments were sometimes mere quibbling or hairsplitting, and a few of them invariably revealed his profound ignorance in certain areas of life and learning and literature, while others betrayed his pet and petty prejudices. You had to wade through these and ignore them, as you did his occasional brief marginal essays on unrelated or completely irrelevant subjects. One or two of his trusted associate editors would sometimes intercept a proof and cross out the impertinent and immaterial Rossisms, but I always insisted that they be left in, for they were the stains and labels of a Ross that never ceased to amuse me.

The blurs and imperfections his scout's eye always caught drew from his pencil such designations as *unclear*, *repetition*, *cliché*, *ellipsis*, and now and then blunter words. He knew when you had tired and were writing carelessly, and when you were "just monkeying around here," or going out on a limb, or writing fancy, or showing off. His

[From the previously mentioned book, *The Years with Ross*.]

"Who he?" became famous not only in the office but outside, and ten years ago was the title of a piece on Ross written by Henry Pringle. Joe Liebling once had "Who he?" painted on the door of his office, to the bewilderment of strangers who wondered what kind of business Liebling could be in. Sometimes this query put a careful finger on someone who had not been clearly identified, and at other times it showed up the gaps in Ross's knowledge of historical, contemporary, or literary figures. (He once said that only two names were familiar to every reader in the civilized world: Houdini and Sherlock Holmes.)

I remember that Ross once told me, after reading a casual of mine, "You must have dropped about eight lines out of this in your final rewrite." The thing ran smoothly enough, it seemed to me when I reread it in his office, but I went back and checked my next to last draft. Ross had been wrong. I had dropped only seven lines.

When he worked on a manuscript or proof, he was surrounded by dictionaries, which he constantly consulted, along with one of his favorite books, Fowler's *Modern English Usage*. He learned more grammar and syntax from Fowler than he had ever picked up in his somewhat sketchy school days. He read the *Oxford English Dictionary* the way other men read fiction, and he sometimes delved into a volume of the *Britannica* at random. One of the funniest moments in Wolcott Gibb's *Season in the Sun* showed the actor who played Ross calmly looking up the word "hurricane" in *Webster's Unabridged* while the advance gales of a real hurricane swept toward him like a cavalry charge.

# H. W. Fowler

## FROM *MODERN ENGLISH USAGE*

### ABSTRACTITIS

THE effect of this disease, now endemic on both sides of the Atlantic, is to make the patient write such sentences as *Participation by the men in the control of the industry is non-existent* instead of *The men have no part in the control of the industry; Early expectation of a vacancy is indicated by the firm* instead of *The firm say they expect to have a vacancy soon; The availability of this material is a diminishing* instead of *This material is getting scarcer; A cessation of dredging has taken place* instead of *Dredging has stopped; Was this the realization of an anticipated liability?* instead of *Did you expect you would have to do this?* And so on, with an abstract word always in command as the subject of the sentence. Persons and what they do, things and what is done to them, are put in the background, and we can only peer at them through a glass darkly. It may no doubt be said that in these examples the meaning is clear enough; but the danger is that, once the disease gets a hold, it sets up a chain reaction. A writer uses abstract words because his thoughts are cloudy; the habit of using them clouds his thoughts still further; he may end by concealing his meaning not only from his readers but also from himself, and writing such sentences as *The actualization of the motiva-*

[From the second edition of *Modern English Usage* by H. W. Fowler. Reprinted by permission of the publisher, The Clarendon Press, Oxford.]

*tion of the forces must to a great extent be a matter of personal angularity.*

The two quotations that follow are instructive examples of the difficulties that readers may find in following the meaning of writers suffering from this disease. The first is English and its subject is the way in which business men arrive at decisions; the second is American and its subject is the testing of foods specially designed for use in certain types of military aircraft, or possibly in space-ships.

1. *Whereas the micro-economic neo-classical theory of distribution was based on a postulate of rationality suited to their static analysis and institutional assumptions, we are no longer justified in accepting this basis and are set the problem of discovering the value premises suited to the expectational analysis and the institutional nature of modern business. The neo-classical postulate of rationality and the concept of the entrepreneur as the profit maximizing individual, should, I think, be replaced by a sociological analysis of the goals of the firm in relation to its nature as an organization within the socio-political system.*

2. *Strangeness of samples has been shown to lead to relative rejection of products in the comparative absence of clues to a frame of reference within which judgement may take place. Variation in clues selected by judges as a basis for evaluation lead to greater inter-judge disagreement. Addition of a functional (utilitarian) basis for judgement tends to reduce relative importance of product physical characteristics as a basis for judgement. In the absence of any judgemental frame of reference reduction in the number of product physical attributes apparent to the judge appears to reduce operation of bases for rejection and increase homogeneity of judgement between subjects; inter-sample discrimination is also reduced.*

\*
\*
\*

ADJECTIVES MISUSED

"An adjective," says the OED, "is a word standing for the name of an attribute which being added to the name of a thing describes the thing more fully and definitely, as a *black coat.*" Adjectives, then, ought to be good friends of the noun. In fact, as has been well said, they have become its enemies. They are often used not to "describe the thing more fully and definitely" but rather to give it some vague and needless intensification or limitation; as if their users thought that the noun by itself was either not impressive enough or too stark, or perhaps even that it was a pity to be content with one word where they might have two. *The operation needs considerable skill and should be performed with proper care. / Effective means of stopping the spread of infection are under active consideration and there is no cause for undue alarm.* The adjective-noun pairs in these sentences are typical of the worser kind of present-day writing, especially business and official. It is clear that *considerable, proper, effective,* and *active* are otiose and *undue* is absurd; their only effect is to undermine the authority of the nouns they are attached to.

*It is my hope that this year concrete and positive steps will be taken to achieve progress towards the union of Africa.* The speaker may perhaps be pardoned for feeling that *steps* needed reinforcing by an adjective; a step may be short or tottery, though it is true that steps of that kind are not likely to "achieve progress." He might reasonably have said *decisive* or *definitive.* He saved himself the trouble of thinking of a suitable adjective by putting in a couple of clichés. One may perhaps walk up concrete steps but one cannot "take" them, and any step must be positive unless indeed it is a step backwards; the speaker cannot have thought it necessary to warn his hearers against thinking that that was what he meant.

The habit of propping up all nouns with adjectives is seen at its worst in those pairs in which the adjective is tautological, adding nothing to the meaning of the noun; such are *grateful thanks, true facts, usual habits, consequent results, definite decisions, unexpected surprise,* and scores of others commonly current. Constant association with an intensifying adjective deprives a noun of the power of standing on its own legs. Thus *danger* must always have its *real,* part its *integral,* and *crisis* its *grave* or *acute,* and *understatements* must be *masterly.* The only hope for a noun thus debilitated is for the combination to be recognized as a cliché and killed by ridicule; there are signs for instance that in this way *test* is ridding itself of *acid* and *moment* of *psychological.*

\*
\*
\*

EUPHEMISM

Means (the use of) a mild or vague or periphrastic expression as a substitute for blunt precision or disagreeable truth. The heyday of euphemism in England was the mid-Victorian era, when the dead were *the departed,* or *no longer living,* pregnant women were *in an interesting condition,* novelists wrote *d———d* for damned and *G—d* for God, bowdlerized editions of Shakespeare and Gibbon were put into the hands of the young and trousers were *nether garments,* or even, jocosely but significantly, *unmentionables* or *inexpressibles.* We are less mealy-mouthed now, though still more given to euphemisms than our Continental neighbours; the notice *Commit no nuisance* or *Decency Forbids* was even in our own day sometimes used for the injunction put more bluntly in France as *Defense d'uriner.* But euphemism is a will-o'-the-wisp for ever eluding pursuit; each new word becomes in turn as explicit as its predecessors and has to be replaced. The most notorious example of the working of this law is that which has given us such a plethora of names for the same thing as *jakes, privy, latrine, water-closet, w.c., lavatory, loo, convenience, ladies, gents, toilet, powder-room, cloaks,* and so on, endlessly. There are of course—or were before the publication of *Lady Chatterley's Lover*—some words, now a small and rapidly diminishing number, too tainted by bawdy and ribaldry to be usable, and for these polite synonyms must be found. But delicacy becomes absurdity when it produces such an anticlimax as is contained in *Pathological tests suggest that she had two blows on the head, was strangled and probably assaulted.* "It is a pity," said a

President of the Probate Divorce and Admiralty Division in 1959, "that plain English is not used about these matters in divorce proceedings. When I say plain English I mean that, so far as I know, ever since the tablets of stone were translated into English in the English version of the Bible, *adultery* has been the word, not *misconduct* or *intimacy* or any other paraphrase of it."

In the present century euphemism has been employed less in finding discreet terms for what is indelicate than as a protective device for governments and as a token of a new approach to psychological and sociological problems. Its value is notorious in totalitarian countries, where assassination and aggression can be made to look respectable by calling them *liquidation* and *liberation*. In Western democracies too use is made of the device of giving things new names in order to improve their appearance. Thus what were at first called crudely Labour Exchanges and Distressed Areas are now *Employment Exchanges* and *Development Districts*: the poor are the *lower income brackets* or the *underprivileged classes*: poor-law relief is *national assistance*; those who used to be known as backward and troublesome children are now *maladjusted*; ladies once termed mistresses itself a euphemism for the earlier *concubines* and *paramours*) are *unmarried wives*; insanity is now *mental disorder*; lunatic asylums are *mental hositals*; criminal lunatics are *Broadmoor patients,* and every kind of unpleasant event that might call for action by the government is discreetly referred to as an EMERGENCY. The same device is used to give a new look to an old occupation. Thus charwomen have become *dailies,* gaolers *prison officers*, commercial travellers *sales representatives,* and RATCATCHERS *rodent operators*. Dustmen, naturally resenting our wounding habit of emphasizing their unlikeness to dukes, are now *refuse collectors* or *street orderlies*; boarding-houses have been rechristened *guest houses*; many butchers call themselves *purveyors of meat* and at least one a *meat technologist*; hairdressers are *tonsorial artists* and undertakers *funeral furnishers* or *directors,* or (U.S.) *morticians.*

\*
\*
\*

## FORMAL WORDS

There are large numbers of words differing from each other in almost all respects, but having this point in common, that they are not the plain English for what is meant, not the forms that the mind uses in its private debates to convey to itself what it is talking about, but translations of these into language that is held more suitable for public exhibition. We tell our thoughts, like our children, to put on their hats and coats before they go out; the policeman who has *gone* to the scene of disturbance will tell the magistrate that he *proceeded* there; a Minister of the Crown may *foresee* the advantages of his policy and *outline* it to his colleagues but in presenting it to Parliament he may *visualize* the first and *adumbrate* the second. These outdoor costumes are often needed; not only may decency be outraged sometimes by over-plain speech; dignity may be compromised if the person who thinks in slang writes also in slang. To the detective who has arrested a receiver of stolen property it comes natural to think and speak of the culprit as a *fence* but that is not what will appear on the charge-sheet. What is intended in this article is not to protest against *all* change of the indoor into the outdoor word, but to point out that the less of such change there is the better. A short haphazard selection of what are to be taken as formal words will put the reader in possession of the point; a full list would run into thousands. It must be observed that no general attack is being made on these words as words; the attack is only on the prevalent notion that the commoner synonyms given after each in brackets ought to be translated into them: *accommodation* (rooms); *adumbrate* (outline); *bear* (carry); *cast* (throw); *cease* (stop); *commence* (begin); *complete* (finish); *conceal* (hide); *desist* (stop); *dispatch* (send off); *donate* (give); *endeavour* (try); *evince* (show); *expedite* (hasten); *extend* (give); *felicitate* (congratulate); *locate* (find); *obtain* (get); *proceed* (go); *purchase* (buy); *remove* (take away); *repast* (meal); *seek* (try, look for); *summon* (send for); *sustain* (suffer); *transmit* (send); *valiant* (brave); *veritable* (true); *vessel* (ship); *visualize* (foresee).

There are very few of our notions that cannot be called by different names; but among these names there is usually one that may be regarded as the thing's proper name, . . . for which another may be substituted to add precision or for many other reasons, but which is present to the mind even behind the substitute. A destroyer is a ship, and, though we never forget its shiphood, the reader is often helped if we call it a destroyer; a vessel is also a ship, but the reader is not usually helped by our calling it a vessel. Though to evince is to show, it does not help him to call showing evincing; what happens is first the translation of *show* into *evince* by the writer, and then the retranslation of *evince* into *show* by the reader. Mind communicates with mind through a veil, and the result is at best dullness, and at worst misunderstanding. The proper name for a notion should not be rejected for another unless the rejector can give some better account to himself of his preference than that he thinks the other will look better in print. If his mental name for a thing is not the proper name, or if, being the proper name, it is also *im*proper, or essentially undignified, let him translate it; but there is nothing to be ashamed of in *buy* or *see* that they should need translating into *purchase* and *observe*; where they give the sense equally well they are fit for any company and need not be shut up at home. Few things contribute more to vigour of style than a practical realization that . . . vernacular or current names are better than the formal words.

*
*
*

## HACKNEYED PHRASES

When *Punch* set down a heading that might be, and very likely has been, the title of a whole book, "Advice to those about to marry," and boiled down the whole contents into a single word, and that a surprise, the thinker of the happy thought deserved congratulations for a week. He hardly deserved immortality, but he has—anonymously, indeed—got it; a large percentage of the great British people cannot think of the dissuasive "don't" without remembering, and, alas! reminding others, of him. There are thousands for whom the only sound sleep is the *sleep of the just*, the light at dusk must always be *dim, religious*; all beliefs are *cherished*, all confidence is *implicit*, all ignorance *blissful*, all isolation *splendid*, all uncertainty *glorious*, all voids *aching*. It would not matter if these associated reflexes stopped at the mind, but they issue by way of the tongue, which is bad, or of the pen, which is worse. King David must surely writhe as often as he hears it told in Sheol what is the latest insignificance that may not be told in Gath. How exasperating it must be for King Canute to be remembered only by those who have forgotten the purpose of his little comedy on the beach. How many a time must Mahomet have regretted his experiment with the mountain as he has heard his acceptance of its recalcitrance once more applied or misapplied! And the witty gentleman who equipped coincidence with her long arm has doubtless suffered even in this life at seeing that arm so mercilessly overworked.

Hackneyed phrases are counted by the hundred, and those registered below are a mere selection. Each of them comes to each of us at some moment in life with, for him, the freshness of novelty upon it; on that occasion it is a delight, and the wish to pass on that delight is amiable. But we forget that of any hundred persons for whom we attempt this good office, though there may be one to whom our phrase is new and bright, it is a stale offence to the ninety and nine.

The purpose with which these phrases are introduced is for the most part that of giving a fillip to a passage that might be humdrum without them. They do serve this purpose with some readers—the less discerning—though with the other kind they more effectually disserve it. But their true use when they come into the writer's mind is as danger-signals; he should take warning that when they suggest themselves it is because what he is writing is bad stuff, or it would not need such help. Let him see to the substance of his cake instead of decorating with sugarplums. In considering the following selection, the reader will bear in mind that he and all of us have our likes and our dislikes in this kind; he may find pet phrases of his own in the list, or miss his pet abominations; he should not on that account decline to accept a caution against the danger of the hackneyed phrase. Acid test. / Balm in Gilead. / Blessing in disguise. / Blushing honours thick upon him. / Clerk of the weather. / Conspicuous by his absence. / Consummation devoutly to be wished. / Cups that cheer but not inebriate. / Curate's egg. / Damn with faint praise. / Defects of his qualities. / Dim religious light. / Explore every avenue. / Fair sex. / Feast of reason. / Few and far between. / Filthy lucre. / Free gratis and for nothing. / Guide philosopher and friend. / Hardy annual. / His own worst enemy. / Ill-gotten gains. / In a Pickwickian sense. / Inner man. / Irony of fate. / Last but not least. / Leave no stone unturned. / Leave severely alone. / Method in his madness. / More in sorrow than in anger. / More sinned against than sinning. / Neither fish flesh nor good red herring. /Neither rhyme nor reason. / Not wisely but too well. / Observed of all observers. / Of that ilk. / Of the —— persuasion. / Olive branches. / Powers that be. / Psychological moment. / Shake the dust from off one's feet. / Sleep the sleep of the just. / Speed the parting guest. / Splendid isolation. / Strain every nerve. / Take one's name in vain. / Tender mercies. / There's the rub. / To be or not to be. / Through thick and thin. / Tower of strength. / Weaker vessel. / Wheels within wheels. / Wise in his generation. / Withers are unwrung.

\*
\*
\*

IF AND WHEN

Any writer who uses this formula lays himself open to entirely reasonable suspicions on the part of his readers. There is the suspicion that he is a mere parrot, who cannot say part of what he has often heard without saying the rest also. There is the suspicion that he likes verbiage for its own sake. There is the suspicion that he is a timid swordsman who thinks he will be safer with a second sword in his left hand. There is the suspicion that he has merely been too lazy to make up his mind between *if* and *when*. Only when the reader is sure enough of his author to know that in his writing none of these probabilities can be true does he turn to the extreme improbability that here at last is a sentence in which *if and when* is really better than *if* or *when* by itself.

This absurdity is so common that it seems worth while to quote some examples, bracketing in each either 'if and' or 'and when', and asking whether the omission would in any way change the meaning or diminish the force of the sentence: *The Radicals do not know quite clearly what they will be at (if and) when the fight is renewed. / It is to be hoped that the Labour Party, if (and when) they come to power, will be courageous enough to free the ether from the bondage of commercialism. / But if (and when) the notices are tendered it will be so arranged that they all terminate on the same day. / Mr. Macmillan should try to come to a preliminary understanding with General de Gaulle about how Britain might dispose of its nuclear armoury if (and when) it joins the common market. / They must, of course, be certain that they are getting what they are bargaining for, but (if and) when they have made sure of that, they would be wisely advised to pay the price.*

It was admitted above that cases were conceivable in which the *if* and the *when* might be genuinely and separately significant. Such cases arise when one desires to say that the result will or does or did not only follow, but follow without delay; they are not in fact rare, and if a really good writer allows himself an *if and when*, one such must have presented itself. But in practice he hardly ever does it even then, because any strong emphasis on the absence of delay is much better given by other means, by the insertion of *at once* or some equivalent in the result clause. So true is this that, when the devotees of *if and when* have had the luck to strike a real opportunity for their favourite, they cannot refrain from inserting some adverb to do over again the work that was the only true function of their *and when;* in the following quotations these adverbs that make *and when* otiose are in roman type: *The electors knew perfectly well that if and when the Parliament Bill was placed on the Statute-book it would* immediately *be used to pass Irish Home Rule.* / *If and when the Unionist Party win a General Election we are to have* at once *a general tariff on foreign manufactured goods.* / *It is true that if and when an amendment giving women the vote is carried this amendment is* thenceforward *to become part and parcel of the Bill.*

*When or if* is not so purposeless as *if and when; or if* does serve to express that the writer, though he expects his condition to be realized, has his doubts: *On official pronouncement as to what particular items of socialist legislation it is proposed to repeal,* when, or if, *the opportunity arrives. As and when* and UNLESS AND UNTIL are open to the same objections as *if and when,* but are much less common.

\*
\*
\*

IRRELEVANT ALLUSION

We all know the people—for they are the majority, and probably include our particular selves—who cannot carry on the ordinary business of everyday talk without the use of phrases containing a part that is appropriate and another that is pointless or worse; the two parts have associated themselves together in their minds as making up what somebody has said, and what others as well as they will find familiar, and they have the sort of pleasure in producing the combination that a child has in airing a newly acquired word. There is indeed a certain charm in the grown-up man's boyish ebullience, not to be restrained by thoughts of relevance from letting the exuberant phrase jet forth. And for that charm we put up with it when one draws our attention to the methodical by telling us there is *method in the madness,* though method and not madness is all there is to see, when another's every winter is *the winter of* his *discontent,* when a third cannot complain of the *light* without calling it *religious* as well as *dim,* when for a fourth nothing can be *rotten* except *in the state of Denmark*, when a fifth, dressed after bathing, tells you that he is *clothed and in his right mind*, or when a sixth, asked whether he does not owe you 4s. 6d. for that cab fare, *owns the soft impeachment*. Other phrases of the kind will be found in the article HACKNEYED PHRASES. A slightly fuller examination of a single example may be useful. The phrase *to leave severely alone* has two reasonable uses: one in the original sense of to leave alone as a method of severe treatment, i.e. to send to Coventry or show contempt for, and the other in contexts where *severely* is to be interpreted by contraries—to leave alone by way not of punishing the object, but of avoiding consequences for the subject. The straightforward meaning and the ironical are both good; anything between them, in which the real meaning is merely to leave alone, and *severely* is no more than an echo, is pointless and vapid and in print intolerable. Examples follow: (1, straightforward) *You must show him, by leaving him severely alone, by putting him into a moral Coventry, your detestation of the crime;* (2, ironical) *Fish of prey do not appear to relish the sharp spines of the stickleback, and usually seem to leave them severely alone;* (3, pointless) *Austria forbids children to smoke in public places; and in German schools and military colleges there are laws upon the subject; France, Spain, Greece, and Portugal, leave the matter severely alone.* It is obvious at once how horrible the faded jocularity of No. 3 is in print; and, though things like it come crowding upon one another in most conversation, they are not very easy to find in newspapers and books of any merit. A small gleaning of them follows: *The moral, as Alice would say, appeared to be that, despite its difference in degree, an obvious essential in the right kind of education had been equally lacking to both these girls* (as Alice, or indeed as you or I, might say). / *Resignation became a virtue of necessity for Sweden* (If you do what you must with a good grace, you make a virtue of necessity; without 'make', *a virtue of necessity* is meaningless). / *I strongly advise the single working-man who would become a suc-*

*cessful backyard poultry-keeper to ignore* the advice of Punch, *and to secure a useful helpmate.* / Like John Brown's soul, *the cricketing family of Edrich goes marching on.* / *The beloved* lustige Wien [merry Vienna] *of his youth had* suffered a sea-change. *The green glacis . . . was blocked by ranges of grand new buildings* (Ariel must chuckle at the odd places in which his *sea change* turns up). / *Some may remember that when the disturbances first occurred the first reaction of the Home Office bore a close resemblance to* Pilate's notorious gesture from the Lithostrotos. (Most will remember what the gesture was; some will remember that St. John tells us that Pilate was sitting in a place called the pavement; all are invited to admire the learning of one who knows that the Greek word translated *pavement* is *lithostrotos*.) / *Many of the celebrities who in that most frivolous of watering-places* do congregate. / *When about to quote Sir Oliver Lodge's tribute to the late leader, Mr. Law drew,* not a dial, *but what was obviously a penny memorandum book from his pocket* (You want to mention that Mr. Bonar Law took a notebook out of his pocket; but pockets are humdrum things; how give a literary touch? Call it a *poke*? no, we can better that; who was it drew what from his poke? Why, Touchstone a dial, to be sure! and there you are).

\*
\*
\*

LITERARY CRITICS' WORDS

The literary critics here meant are not the writers of books or treatises or essays of which the substance is criticism; readers of that form of literature are a class apart, and if a special lingo exists between them and its writers, the rest of us are not concerned to take exception to it. Anything said in this book about literary critics is aimed only at the newspaper reviewers of books and other works of art. Those reviewers, as anyone knows who examines them critically in their turn, give us work that ranges from the very highest literary skill (if the power of original creation is set aside as here irrelevant) to the merest hack-work. The point is that, whether they are highly accomplished writers, or tiros employed on the theory that anyone is good enough to pass an opinion on a book, their audience is not the special class that buys critical works because its tastes are literary, but the general public, which buys its criticism as part of its newspaper, and does not know the critics' lingo. It follows that, the better the critic, the fewer literary critics' words he uses. The good critic is aware that his public wants to understand, and he has no need to convince it that he knows what he is talking about by parading words that it does not understand. With the inferior critic the establishment of his status is the first consideration, and he effects it by so using, let us say, *actuality, engaged,* and *inevitable,* that the reader shall become aware of a mysterious difference between the sense attaching to the words in ordinary life and the sense now presented to him. He has taken *actuality* to mean actualness or reality; the critic perplexes him by giving it another sense, which it has a right to in French, where *actuel* means present, but not in English—the sense of up-to-dateness, or resemblance not to truth in general but to present-day conditions; and he does this without mentioning that he is gallicizing. And so with the other words; the reader is to have it borne in upon him that a more instructed person than himself is talking to him even if it means coining a new word; *cretinocratic,* for instance, is the term by which one reviewer, evidently a very superior person, expresses his opinion of television programmes. One mark of the good literary critic is that he is able to explain his meaning without resort to these lingo words and under no necessity to use them as advertisements.

\*
\*
\*

### LONG VARIANTS

"The better the writer, the shorter his words" would be a statement needing many exceptions for individual persons and particular subjects; but for all that it would be broadly true, especially about English writers. Those who run to long words are mainly the unskilful and tasteless; they confuse pomposity with dignity, flaccidity with ease, and bulk with force; see LOVE OF THE LONG WORD. A special form of long word is now to be illustrated. When a word for the notion wanted exists, some people (1) forget or do not know that word, and make up another from the same stem with an extra suffix or two; or (2) are not satisfied with a mere current word, and resolve to decorate it, also with an extra suffix; or (3) have heard a longer form that resembles it, and are not aware that this other form is appropriated to another sense. Cases of (1) and (2) are often indistinguishable; the motive differs, but the result is the same; and they will here be mixed together, those of (3) being kept apart.

(1) and (2). Needless lengthenings of established words due to oversight or caprice: administrate (administer); assertative (assertive); contumacity (contumacy); cultivatable (cultivable); dampen (damp, v.); denunciate (denounce); dubiety (doubt); epistolatory (epistolary); experimentalize (experiment, v.); extemporaneously (ex tempore); filtrate (filter, v.); preventative (preventive); quieten (quiet, v.); transportation (transport).

Examples: *The capability of the Germans to* administrate *districts with a mixed population.* / *Still speaking in a very loud* assertative *voice, he declared that . . .* / *Mlle St Pierre's affected interference provoked* contumacity. / *If you add to the* cultivatable *lands of the immediate Rhine valley those of . . .* / *His extreme sensitiveness to all the suggestions which* dampen *enthusiasm . . .* / *Lord Lansdowne has done the Liberal Party a good turn by putting Tariff Reform to the front; about this there can be no* dubiety. / *Cowper's Letters . . . the best example of the* epistolatory *art our language possesses.* / *A few old masters that have been* experimentalized *on.* / *M. Delcassé, speaking* extemporaneously *but with notes, said . . .* / *A Christianity* filtrated *of all its sectional dogmas.* / *Jamaica ginger, which is a very good* preventative *of seasickness.* /

*Whether that can be attributed to genuine American support or to a* quietening *down of the speculative position is a matter of some doubt.*

3. Wrong use of longer forms due to confusion: advancement (advance); alternative (alternate); correctitude (correctness); creditable (credible); definitive (definite); distinctive (distinct); estimation (estimate); evaluate (value); excepting (except); intensive (intense); partially (partly); prudential (prudent); reverential (reverent); transcendental (transcendent). The differences of meaning between the longer and shorter words are not here discussed, but will be found, unless too familiar to need mention, under the words in their dictionary places.

Examples: *It was only by* advancement *of money to the tenant farmers that the calamity could be ended.* / *When the army is not fully organized, when it is in process of* alternative *disintegration and rally, the problems are insoluble.* / *Baron —— believes himself to be the oldest living Alsatian; and there is small reason to doubt the* correctitude *of his belief.* / *It is* creditably *stated that the length of line dug and wired in the time is near a record.* / *But warning and suggestion are more in evidence than* definitive *guidance.* / *Trade relations of an ordinary kind are quite* distinctive *from those having annexation as their aim.* / *Since November 11 the Allies have been able to form a* precise estimation *of Germany's real intentions.* / *The sojourn of belligerent ships in French waters has never been limited* excepting *by certain clearly defined rules.* / *The covered flowers being less* intensively *coloured than the others.* / *The two feet, branching out into ten toes, are* partially *of iron and* partially *of clay.* / *It is often a very easy thing to act* prudentially, *but alas! too often only after we have toiled to our prudence through a forest of delusions.* / *Their behaviour in church was anything but* reverential. / *The matter is of* transcendental *importance, especially in the present disastrous state of the world.*

It only remains to say that nothing in this article must be taken as countenancing the shortening of such words as *quantitative* and *authoritative;* and see INTERPRE(TA)TIVE. *It is as if the* quantitive *theory of naval strategy held the field.* / *Her finely finished* authoritive *performance was of great value.*

\*
\*
\*

### LOVE OF THE LONG WORD

It need hardly be said that shortness is a merit in words. There are often reasons why shortness is not possible; much less often there are occasions when length, not shortness, is desirable. But it is a general truth that the short words are not only handier to use, but more powerful in effect; extra syllables reduce, not increase, vigor. This is particularly so in English, where the native words are short, and the long words are foreign.

\*
\*
\*

### MIXED METAPHORS

*This is not the time to* throw up the sponge, *when the enemy, already weakened and divided, are* on the run to a new defensive position. A mixture of prize-ring and battlefield. / *The Rt. Hon. Gentleman is leading the people over the precipice with his head in the sand.* A strange confusion between the behaviour of Gadarene swine and that of ostriches. / *There is every indication that Nigeria will be a tower of strength and will forge ahead.* A mixture of a fortress and a ship. / *The Avon and Dorset River Board should not act like King Canute, bury its head in the sands, and ride rough-shod over the interests of those who live by the land and enjoy their fishing.* (A picture that staggers the imagination, and a libel on a great king.)

In the following extract from a speech it is difficult to be sure how many times metaphors are mixed; readers versed in the mysteries of oscillation may be able to decide: *No society, no community, can place its house in such a condition that it is always* on a rock, oscillating *between solvency and insolvency. What I have to do is to see that our house is* built upon a solid foundation, *never allowing the possibility of the Society's* lifeblood being sapped. *Just in proportion as you are careful in looking after the condition of your income, just in proportion as you deal with them carefully, will the solidarity of the Society's financial condition remain intact. Immediately you begin to* play fast and loose *with your income* the first blow *at your financial stability will have been struck.*

*
*
*

NEW VERBS IN -IZE

A feature of the second Elizabethan age, as of the first, is that new words proliferate. One way of making them is to add the suffix -*ize* to a noun or adjective, and so increase our stock of verbs. The device itself is far from new; our vocabulary already contains some hundreds of verbs so formed. The Greeks used [a] suffix . . . to make verbs with, and we have followed them; sometimes we take over what is, except for its termination, an actual Greek word (*apologize, dogmatize, ostracize,* etc.); sometimes we add -*ize* to a word or stem, usually of Greek or Latin origin (*colonize, immunize, summarize,* etc.) but occasionally of later date (*bastardize, jeopardize, standardize,* etc.) especially to names of places or people (*americanize, bowdlerize, galvanize, pasteurize,* etc.). Within reason it is a useful and unexceptionable device, but it is now being employed with a freedom beyond reason. The purpose is usually to enable us to say in one word what would otherwise need more than one. Whether that justifies the creation of a new -*ize* word is a question on which opinions will differ, and it does not admit of a categorical answer.

Most verbs in -*ize* are inelegant. Sir Alan Herbert has compared them to lavatory fittings, useful in their proper place but not to be multiplied beyond what is necessary for practical purposes.

*
*
*

98

## NOVELTY HUNTING

It is a confession of weakness to cast about for words of which one can feel not that they give one's meaning more intelligibly or exactly than those the man in the street would have used in expressing the same thing, but that they are not the ones that would have occurred to him. Anyone can say *surroundings* and *combination* and *total*; I will say *ambience* and *synthesis* and *overall*. Anyone can say *mixed feelings* and *shock* and *workable*; I will say *ambivalence* and *trauma* and *viable*. Everyone is talking about *angry young men*; I will call them *professional iracunds*. Why? Obviously because, there being nothing new in what I have to say, I must make up for its staleness by something new in the way I say it. And if that were all, if each novelty-hunter struck out a line for himself, we could be content to register novelty-hunting as a useful outward sign of inward dullness, and leave such writers carefully alone. Unluckily they hunt in packs, and when one of them has a find they are all in full cry after it, till it becomes a VOGUE WORD, to the great detriment of the language.

\*
\*
\*

## OFFICIALESE

is a pejorative term for a style of writing marked by peculiarities supposed to be characteristic of officials. If a single word were needed to describe those peculiarities, that chosen by Dickens, *circumlocution*, is still the most suitable. They may be ascribed to a combination of causes: a feeling that plain words sort ill with the dignity of office, a politeness that shrinks from blunt statement, and, above all, the knowledge that for those engaged in the perilous game of politics, and their servants, vagueness is safer than precision. The natural result is a stilted and verbose style, not readily intelligible—a habit of mind for instance that automatically rejects the adjective *unsightly* in favour of the periphrasis *detrimental to the visual amenities of the locality*.

\*
\*
\*

OUT OF THE FRYING-PAN

A very large proportion of the mistakes that are made in writing result neither from simple ignorance nor from carelessness, but from the attempt to avoid what are rightly or wrongly taken to be faults of grammar or style. The writer who produces an ungrammatical, an ugly, or even a noticeably awkward phrase, and lets us see that he has done it in trying to get rid of something else that he was afraid of, gives a worse impression of himself than if he had risked our catching him in his original misdemeanour; he is out of the frying-pan into the fire. A few typical examples will be here collected, with references to other articles in which the tendency to mistaken correction is set forth more at large.

*Recognition is given to it by no matter whom it is displayed.* The frying-pan was "no matter whom it is displayed by", which the writer did not dare keep, with its preposition at end; but in his hurry he jumped into nonsense; see . . . PREPOSITION AT END. / *When the record of this campaign comes dispassionately to be written, and in just perspective, it will be found that . . .* The writer took "to be dispassionately written" for a SPLIT INFINITIVE, and by his correction convinces us that he does not know a split infinitive when he sees it. / *In the hymn and its setting there is something which, to use a word of Coleridge, "finds" men.* "A word of Coleridge's" is an idiom whose genesis may be doubtful, but it has the advantage over the correction of being English; *a word of Coleridge* is no more English than *a friend of me.* . . . / *But the badly cut-up enemy troops were continually reinforced and substituted by fresh units.* The frying-pan was REPLACE in the sense "take the place of"; the fire is the revelation that the writer has no idea what the verb SUBSTITUTE means. / *Sir Starr Jameson has had one of the most varied and picturesque careers of any Colonial statesmen.* "Of any statesman", idiomatic but apparently illogical, has been corrected to what is neither logical (*of all* would have been nearer to sense) nor English. / *The claim yesterday was for the difference between the old rate, which was a rate by agree-*

*ment, and between the new.* The writer feared, with some contempt for his readers' intelligence, that they would not be equal to carrying on the construction of *between;* he has not mended matters by turning sense into nonsense. *. . . / The reception was held at the bride's aunt.* The reporter was right in disliking *bride's aunt's,* but should have found time to think of "at the house of".

The impression must not be left, however, that it is fatal to read over and correct what one has written. The moral is that correction requires as much care as the original writing, or more; the slapdash corrector, who should not be in such a hurry, and the uneducated corrector, who should not be writing at all, are apt to make things worse than they found them.

*
*
*

SENTRY PARTICIPLE ETC.

If newspaper editors, in the interest of their readers, maintain any discipline over the gentlemen who provide inch-long paragraphs, they should take measures against a particular form that, by a survival of the unfittest, bids fair to swallow up all others. In these paragraphs, before we are allowed to enter, we are challenged by the sentry in the guise of a participle or some equivalent posted in advance to secure that our interview with the C.O. (or subject of the sentence) shall not take place without due ceremony. The fussiness of this is probably entertaining while it is quite fresh; one cannot tell, because it is no longer fresh to anyone. It is likely to result in jamming together two unrelated ideas in one sentence. Examples: *Described as "disciples of Tolstoi", two Frenchmen sentenced at Cheltenham to two months' imprisonment for false statements to the registration officer are not to be recommended for deportation. / Winner of many rowing trophies, Mr. Robert George Dugdale, aged seventy-five, died at Eton. / Believed to be the youngest organist in the country, Master Herbert Woolverton, who officiates at Hutton Church, Essex, has passed the examination as Asso-*

*ciate of . . . / Thirty-four years in the choir of the Chapel Royal, Hampton Court Palace, Mr. Francis P. Hill, of Milner Road, Kingston, has retired. / Found standing in play astride the live rail of the electric line at Willesden and in danger of instant death, Walter Spentaford, twelve, was fined 12s. for trespass.* The device of the sentry participle is now worked so hard that the participle is liable to become UNATTACHED, though it cannot often be left in the air quite so egregiously as are the two participles in this description of the departure of Grivas from Cyprus. *Seen off at Nicosia airport by the head of the security forces which had failed to track him, boastfully claiming that he had spent his time "with the British", seldom has an Imperial Power looked so ridiculous.*

\*
\*
\*

THE IMPERSONAL PASSIVE

*it is felt, it is thought, it is believed,* etc.—is a construction dear to those who write official and business letters. It is reasonable enough in statements made at large—*It is believed that a large green car was in the vicinity at the time of the accident. / It is understood that the wanted man is wearing a raincoat and a cloth cap.* But when one person is addressing another it often amounts to a pusillanimous shrinking from responsibility (*It is felt that your complaint arises from a misunderstanding. / It is thought that ample provision has been made against this contingency*). The person addressed has a right to know who it is that entertains a feeling he may not share or a thought he may consider mistaken, and is justly resentful of the suggestion that it exists in the void. On the other hand, the impersonal passive should have been used in *For these reasons the effects of the American recession upon Britain will be both smaller and shorter than were originally feared. Were* should be *was* (i.e. than it was originally feared they would be).

\*
\*
\*

### DOUBLE PASSIVES

*The point is sought to be evaded:* monstrosities of this kind, which are as repulsive to the grammarian as to the stylist, perhaps spring by false analogy from the superficially similar type seen in *The man was ordered to be shot.* But the forms from which they are developed are dissimilar: They ordered the man *to be shot,* but They seek *to evade* the point; whereas *man* is one member of the double-barrelled object of *ordered, point* is the object not of *seek* at all, but of *evade.* It follows that, although *man* can be made subject of the passive *was ordered* while its fellow-member is deferred, *point* cannot be made subject of the passive *is sought,* never having been in any sense the object of *seek.*

To use this clumsy and incorrect construction in print amounts to telling the reader that he is not worth writing readable English for; a speaker may find himself compelled to resort to it because he must not stop to recast the sentence he has started on, but writers have no such excuse. Some of the verbs most maltreated in this way are *attempt, begin, desire, endeavour, hope, intend, propose, purpose, seek,* and *threaten* (commonest of all perhaps is *fear* in such a sentence as *all the passengers are feared to have been killed* or *feared killed;* so common as to qualify as a STURDY INDEFENSIBLE). A few examples follow: *Now that the whole is attempted to be systematized. / The mystery was assiduously, though vainly, endeavoured to be discovered. / The darkness of the house (forgotten to be opened, though it was long since day) yielded to the glare. / A process whereby a tangle of longlasting problems is striven to be made gradually better. / A new definition of a drunkard was sought to be inserted into the Bill.* In legal or quasi-legal language this construction may sometimes be useful and unexceptionable: *Diplomatic privilege applies only to such things as are done or omitted to be done in the course of a person's official duties. / Motion made: that the words proposed to be left out stand part of the Question.* But that is no excuse for admitting it to literary English.

\*
\*
\*

PREPOSITION AT END

It was once a cherished superstition that prepositions must be kept true to their name and placed before the word they govern in spite of the incurable English instinct for putting them late ("They are the fittest timber to make great politics *of*" said Bacon; and "What are you hitting me *for?*" says the modern schoolboy). "A sentence ending in a preposition is an inelegant sentence" represents what used to be a very general belief, and it is not yet dead. One of its chief supports is the fact that Dryden, an acknowledged master of English prose, went through all his prefaces contriving away the final prepositions that he had been guilty of in his first editions. It is interesting to find Ruskin almost reversing this procedure. In the text of the *Seven Lamps* there is a solitary final preposition to be found, and no more; but in the later footnotes they are not avoided (*Any more wasted words . . . I never heard of. / Men whose occupation for the next fifty years would be the knocking down every beautiful building they could lay their hands on*). Dryden's earlier practice shows him following the English instinct; his later shows him sophisticated with deliberate latinism: "I am often put to a stand in considering whether what I write be the idiom of the tongue, . . . and have no other way to clear my doubts but by translating my English into Latin." The natural inference from this would be: you cannot put a preposition (roughly speaking) later than its word in Latin, and therefore you must not do so in English. Gibbon improved upon the doctrine, and, observing that prepositions and adverbs are not always easily distinguished, kept on the safe side by not ending sentences with *on, over, under,* or the like, even when they would have been adverbs.

The fact is that the remarkable freedom enjoyed by English in putting its prepositions late and omitting its relatives is an important element in the flexibility of the language. The power of saying *A state of dejection such as they are absolute strangers to* (Cowper) instead of *A state of dejection of an intensity to which they are absolute strangers,* or *People worth talking to* instead of *People with whom it is worth while to talk,* is not one to be lightly surrendered. But the Dryden-Gibbon tradition has remained in being, and even now immense pains are sometimes expended in changing spontaneous into artificial English. *That depends on what they are cut with* is not improved by conversion into *That depends on with what they are cut;* and too often the lust of sophistication, once blooded, becomes uncontrollable, and ends with, *That depends on the answer to the question as to with what they are cut.* Those who lay down the universal principle that final prepositions are "inelegant" are unconsciously trying to deprive the English language of a valuable idiomatic resource, which has been used freely by all our greatest writers except those whose instinct for English idiom has been overpowered by notions of correctness derived from Latin standards. The legitimacy of the prepositional ending in literary English must be uncompromisingly maintained; in respect of elegance or inelegance, every example must be judged not by any arbitrary rule, but on its own merits, according to the impression it makes on the feeling of educated English readers.

In avoiding the forbidden order, unskilful handlers of words often fall into real blunders (see OUT OF THE FRYING-PAN). A few examples of bad grammar obviously due to this cause may fairly be offered without any suggestion that a rule is responsible for all blunders made in attempting to keep it. The words in brackets indicate the avoided form, which is not necessarily the best, but is at least better than that substituted for it: *The War Office does not care, the Disposal Board is indifferent, and there is no one* on whom *to fix the blame or* to hang (no one to fix the blame on or to hang). / *The day begins with a ride with the wife and as many others as want to ride and* for whom *there is horseflesh available* (and as there are horses for). / *This was a memorable expedition in every way, greatly appreciated by the Japanese, the Sinhalese, the Siamese, and* with whomever *else B.O.A.C. briefly deposited their valuable cargo* (and whomever else B.O.A.C. briefly deposited their valuable cargo with). / *It is like the art* of which

*Huysmans dreamed* but *never* executed (the art that Huysmans dreamed of). / *That promised land* for which *he was to prepare, but scarcely* to enter (that he was to prepare for).

It was said above that almost all our great writers have allowed themselves to end a sentence or a clause with a preposition. A score or so of specimens follow ranging over six centuries, to which may be added the Bacon, Cowper, and Ruskin examples already given: (Chaucer) But yit to this thing ther is yit another thing y-ijoigned, more to ben wondred upon. (Spenser) Yet childe ne kinsman living had he none To leave them to. (Shakespeare) Such bitter business as the day Would quake to look on. (Jonson) Prepositions follow sometimes the nouns they are coupled with. (Bible) I will not leave thee, until I have done that which I have spoken to thee of. (Milton) What a fine conformity would it starch us all into. (Burton) Fit for Calphurnius and Democritus to laugh at. (Pepys) There is good ground for what he goes about. (Congreve) And where those qualities are, 'tis pity they should want objects to shine upon. (Swift) The present argument is the most abstracted that ever I engaged in. (Defoe) Avenge the injuries . . . by giving them up to the confusions their madness leads them to. (Burke) The less convincing on account of the party it came from. (Lamb) Enforcing his negation with all the might . . . he is master of. (De Quincey) The average, the prevailing tendency, is what we look at. (Landor) The vigorous mind has mountains to climb, and valleys to repose in. (Hazlitt) It does for something to talk about. (Peacock) Which they would not otherwise have dreamed of. (Mill) We have done the best that the existing state of human reason admits of. (Kinglake) More formidable than any . . . that Ibrahim Pasha had to contend with. (M. Arnold) Let us see what it amounts to. (Lowell) Make them show what they are made of. (Thackeray) So little do we know what we really are after. (Kipling) Too horrible to be trifled with.

If it were not presumptuous, after that, to offer advice, the advice would be this: Follow no arbitrary rule, but remember that there are often two or more possible arrangements between which a choice should be consciously made. If the final preposition that has naturally presented itself sounds comfortable, keep it; if it does not sound comfortable, still keep it if it has compensating vigour, or when among awkward possibilities it is the least awkward. If the "preposition" is in fact the adverbial particle of a PHRASAL VERB, no choice is open to us; it cannot be wrested from its partner. Not even Dryden could have altered *which I will not put up with* to *up with which I will not put*.

\*
\*
\*

## QUOTATION

Didactic and polemical writers quote passages from others to support themselves by authority or to provide themselves with something to controvert; critics quote from the books they review in illustration of their estimates. These are matters of business on which no general advice need be offered. But the literary or decorative quotation is another thing. A writer expresses himself in words that have been used before because they give his meaning better than he can give it himself, or because they are beautiful or witty, or because he expects them to touch a chord of association in his reader, or because he wishes to show that he is learned or well read. Quotations due to the last motive are invariably ill advised. The discerning reader detects it and is contemptuous; the undiscerning is perhaps impressed, but even then is at the same time repelled, pretentious quotations being the surest road to tedium. The less experienced a writer is, and therefore on the whole the less well read he is also, the more is he tempted to this error. The experienced knows he had better avoid it; and the well-read, aware that he could quote if he would, is not afraid that readers will think he cannot. Quoting for association's sake has more chance of success, or at any rate less certainty of failure; but it needs a homogeneous audience. If a jest's prosperity lies in the ear of him that hears it, so too does a quotation's; to each reader those quotations are agreeable that neither strike him as hackneyed nor rebuke his ignorance by their complete novelty, but rouse dormant memories. Quotation, then, should be adapted to the probable reader's degree of cultivation, which presents a very pretty problem to those who have a mixed audience to face; the less mixed the audience, the safer is it to quote for association. Lastly, the sayings wise or witty or beautiful with which it may occur to us to adorn our own inferior matter, not for business, not for benefit of clergy, not for charm of association, but as carvings on a cathedral façade, or pictures on the wall, or shells in a bower-bird's run, have we the skill to choose and place them? Are we architects, or bric-à-brac dealers, or what?

Enough has perhaps been said to indicate generally the dangers of quoting. A few examples follow of oddities that may serve as particular warnings; see also IRRELEVANT ALLUSION.

Pretentiousness: *In the summer of 1867 England received with strange welcome a strange visitor.* "Quis novus his nostris successit sedibus hospes?" *Looking forward into the future we may indeed apply yet other words of Dido, and say of the new comer to these shores* "Quibus ille jactatus fatis!" *It was the Sultan of Turkey who came to visit England.*

Manglings: *It may seem somewhat unfair to quote the saying of the old Latin poet,* "Montes parturiunt, ridiculus mus est", *in relation to the Government's achievements in matters of domestic legislation.* (Something seems to have happened to the old Latin poet's metre and tense.) / *His treatment of the old, old story of the Belgian franc-tireur is typical.* "L'animal est très méchant, il se défend quand on l'attaque." (Something has happened to the French poet's rhyme, as well as his metre.) / *Here again, however, there was a fly in the amber—the incoming of the Italians.* (A fly in amber, or a fly in the ointment—what can it matter?) / *The Chancellor of the Exchequer finds himself on the horns of a quandary.* (A quandary is no doubt an awkward place to get out of but not because of a fear of impaling oneself on any horns.)

Quotation sandwich: *Yet if we take stock of our situation today, even those of us who are "fearful saints" can afford "fresh courage" to "take." / The "pigmy body" seemed "fretted to decay" by the "fiery soul" within it.* (Original: A fiery soul which, working out its way, Fretted the pigmy body to decay.)

Foreign oil and English water: *Who will be pleased to send details to all who are interested in strengthening l'entente cordiale.* (Read *the* entente cordiale.) / *Even if a change were desirable with Kitchener duce et auspice. / Salmasius alone was not unworthy sublimi flagello. / The feeling that one is an antecedentem scelestum. / The clergy in rochet, alb, and other best pontificalibus.*

Clumsy adaptation: *But the problem of inducing a refractory camel to squeeze himself through the eye of an inconvenient needle is and remains insoluble. / Modern fashions do not presuppose an uncorseted figure; that way would modish disaster lie. / Gossip on a subject which is still on the knees of the future.*

\*
\*
\*

RHYTHM

Rhythmless speech or writing is like the flow of liquid from a pipe or tap; it runs with smooth monotony from when it is turned on to when it is turned off, provided it is clear stuff; if it is turbid, the smooth flow is queerly and abruptly checked from time to time, and then resumed. Rhythmic speech or writing is like waves of the sea, moving onward with alternating rise and fall, connected yet separate, like but different, suggestive of some law, too complex for analysis or statement, controlling the relations between wave and wave, waves and sea, phrase and phrase, phrases and speech. In other words, live speech, said or written is rhythmic, and rhythmless speech is at the best dead. The rhythm of verse is outside the scope of this book, and that of prose cannot be considered in its endless detail; but a few words upon it may commend the subject as worth attention to some of those who are stirred by the mere name to ribald laughter at faddists and aesthetes.

A sentence or a passage is rhythmical if, when said aloud, it falls naturally into groups of words each well fitted by its length and intonation for its place in the whole and its relation to its neighbours. Rhythm is not a matter of counting syllables and measuring the distance between accents; to that misconception is due the ridicule sometimes cast upon it by sensible people conscious of producing satisfactory English but wrongly thinking they do it without the aid of rhythm. They will tell you that they see to it, of course, that their sentences sound right, and that is enough for them; but, if their seeing to it is successfully done, it is because they are, though they do not realize it, masters of rhythm. For, while rhythm does not mean counting syllables and measuring accent-intervals, it does mean so arranging the parts of your whole that each shall enhance, or at the least not detract from, the general effect upon the ear; and what is that but seeing to it that your sentences sound right? Metre is measurement; rhythm is flow, a flow with pulsations as infinitely various as the shape and size and speed of the waves; and infinite variety is not amenable to tabulation such as can be applied to metre. So it is that the prose writer's best guide to rhythm is not his own experiments in, or other people's rules for, particular cadences and stress-schemes, but an instinct for the difference between what sounds right and what sounds wrong. It is an instinct cultivable by those on whom nature has not bestowed it, but on one condition only—that they will make a practice of reading aloud. That test soon divides matter, even for a far from sensitive ear, into what reads well and what reads tamely, haltingly, jerkily, lopsidedly, topheavily, or otherwise badly; the first is the rhythmical, the other the rhythmless. By the time the reader aloud has discovered that in a really good writer every sentence is rhythmical, while bad writers perpetually offend or puzzle his ear—a discovery, it is true, not very quickly made—he is capable of passing judgement on each of his own sentences if he will be at the pains to read them, too, aloud. In all this, reading aloud need not be taken quite literally; there is an art of tacit reading aloud ("My own voice pleased me, and still more the mind's Internal echo of the imperfect sound"), reading with the eye and not the mouth, that is, but being as fully aware of the unuttered sound as of the sense.

* <br> * <br> *

SOCIOLOGESE

We live in a scientific age, and like to show, by the words we use, that we think in a scientific way. In more than one article of this dictionary, . . . reference is made to the harm that is being done to the language by this well-meant ambition. . . . Sociologese . . . deserves an article to itself. Sociology is a new science concerning itself not with esoteric matters outside the comprehension of the layman, as the older sciences do, but with the ordinary affairs of ordinary people. This seems to engender in those who write about it a feeling that the law of any abstruseness in their subject demands a compensatory abstruseness in their language. Thus, in the field of industrial relations, what the ordinary man would call an informal talk may be described as *a relatively unstructured conversational interaction*, and its purpose may be said to be *to build, so to speak, within the mass of demand and need, a framework of limitation recognized by both worker and client*. This seems to mean that the client must be persuaded that, beyond a certain point, he can only rely on what used to be called self-help; but that would not sound a bit scientific. Or again, still in the field of industrial relations, results may be summarized in language like this: *The technique here reported resulted from the authors' continuing interest in human variables associated with organizational effectiveness. Specifically, this technique was developed to identify and analyse several types of interpersonal activities and relations, and to provide a method for expressing the degree of congruence between two or more of these activities and relations in indices which might be associated with available criteria of organizational effectiveness.*

There are of course writers on sociological subjects who express themselves clearly and simply; that makes it the more deplorable that such books are often written in a jargon which one is almost tempted to believe is deliberately employed for the purpose of making what is simple appear complicated, exhibiting in an extreme form the common vice (see ABSTRACTITIS) of preferring pretentious abstract words to simple concrete ones. It would be easy but tedious to multiply examples; two will be enough.

1. (On the reason why the "middle class" speak differently from the "lower working class".) *The typical, dominant speech-mode of the middle class is one where speech becomes an object of perceptual activity, and a "theoretical attitude" is developed towards the structural possibilities of sentence organization. This speech-mode facilitates the verbal elaboration of subjective intent, sensitivity to the implications of separateness and difference, and point to the possibilities inherent in a complex conceptual hierarchy for the organization of experience. [The lower working class] are limited to a form of language use which, though allowing for a vast range of possibilities, provides a speech form which discourages the speaker from verbally elaborating subjective intent, and progressively orients the user to descriptive rather than abstract concepts.*

2. (On family life.) *The home then is the specific zone of functional potency that grows about a live parenthood; a zone at the periphery of which is an active interfacial membrane or surface furthering exchange—from within outwards and from without inwards—a mutualising membrane between the family and the society in which it lives.*

\*
\*
\*

## UNATTACHED PARTICIPLES

and adjectives (or wrongly attached). A firm sent in its bill with the following letter: *Dear Sir, We beg to enclose herewith statement of your account for goods supplied, and being desirous of clearing our Books to end May will you kindly favour us with cheque in settlement per return, and much oblige.* The reply ran: *Sirs, You have been misinformed. I have no wish to clear your books.* It may be hoped that the desire on which they based their demand was ultimately (though not per return) satisfied, but they had certainly imputed it to the wrong person by seeming to attach *being desirous* not to the pronoun it belonged to *(we)*, but to another *(you)*. The duty of so arranging one's sentences that they will stand grammatical analysis is much more generally recognized than it formerly was, and it is now not a sufficient defence for looseness of this kind to produce parallels, as can very easily be done, even from great writers of past generations. . . .

\*
\*
\*

## UNEQUAL YOKEFELLOWS

The phrase is here used in a comprehensive sense enabling a number of faults, most of them treated at length in other articles, to be exhibited side by side as varieties of one species. They are all such as do not obstruct seriously the understanding of the passages in which they occur, but they do inflict a passing discomfort on fastidious readers. For a writer who is not fastidious it is an irksome task to keep in mind the readers who are, and he inclines to treat symmetry as troublesome or even obtrusive formalism; he too could be mechanically regular if he would, but he is not going to be at the pains of revising his first draft into conformity with niceties that are surely of no consequence. It is true that such revising is an ungrateful task; but there must be something wrong with a writer who, by the time he is through his apprenticeship, is not free of the need for this sort of revision; to shape one's sentences aright as one puts them down, instinctively

113

avoiding lopsidedness and checking all details of the framework, is not the final crown of an accomplished writer, but part of the rudiments of his trade. If one has neglected to acquire that habit in early days, one has no right to grumble at the choice that later confronts one between slovenliness and revision.

Conspicuous among the slights commonly inflicted upon the minor symmetries are those illustrated below:

*Scarcely* (temporal) demands *when* or *before: Scarcely was the drain finished* than *several sickened with diphtheria.* . . .

*Each* demands a singular verb: *The opportunities which each* are *capable of turning to account.* . . .

Only the expressed part of a verb used with one auxiliary can be "understood" with another: *Examples of false and exaggerated reports have always and will always disturb us.* . . .

A subjunctive in one of two parallel clauses demands a subjunctive in the other: *If the appeal* be *made and* results *in.* . . .

Sealing up of a subject within its verb demands repetition of the subject if it is to serve again: *Does he dislike its methods and will only mention* . . . ?

One or two other types may be added without references: *Either he did not know or was lying* (read *He either*); *The old one was as good if not better than this* (read *as good as this if not better*); *One of the worst kings that* has *ever reigned* (read *have*); *It is all and more than* I expected (read *all I expected, and more*); *He was young, rich, handsome, and enjoyed life* (read *and handsome.* . . .

*<br>*<br>*

## VULGARIZATION

Many words depend for their legitimate effect upon rarity; when blundering hands are laid upon them and they are exhibited in unsuitable places, they are vulgarized. *Save* (prep.) and *ere* were formerly seldom seen in prose, but, when seen, they then consorted well with any passage of definitely elevated style, lending to it and receiving from it the dignity that was proper to them. Things are now so different that the elevated style shuns them as tawdry ornament; it says what the man in the street says, *before* and *except*, and leaves *ere* and *save* to those writers who have not yet ceased to find them beautiful—which is naturally confusing, and an injury to the language. The fate of *awful* . . . is of rather earlier date, but is still remembered, and *weird* and *ghastly* have, almost in our own century, been robbed of all their weirdness and ghastliness. There is little in common between the LYRICS of Pindar and those of a modern "musical," or between the *cartoons* of Raphael and the strip variety of our popular press, or between the SATIRES of Juvenal and much of what goes by that name today, or between the SAGA of Grettir the Strong and that of Flook. One would like to represent to the gossip writers and advertisers that they are desecrating the words EPIC, *glamorous*, and FABULOUS by applying them to cocktail parties, cosmetics, and strip-tease girls; but they would probably be as indignant at the notion that their touch pollutes as the writer would be who was told that he was injuring *faerie* and *evanish* and *mystic* and *optimistic* and *unthinkable* and *replica* by selecting them in honourable preference to *fairy* and *vanish* and *mysterious* and *hopeful* and *incredible* and *copy*. Vulgarization of words that should not be in common use robs some of their aroma, others of their substance, others again of their precision; but nobody likes to be told that the best service he can do to a favourite word is to leave it alone, and perhaps the less said here on this matter the better. . . .

*
*
*

WORKING AND STYLISH WORDS

No one, unless he has happened upon this article at a very early stage of his acquaintance with this book, will suppose that the word *stylish* is meant to be laudatory. Nor is it; but neither is this selection of stylish words to be taken for a blacklist of out-and-out undesirables. Many of them are stylish only when they are used in certain senses, being themselves in other senses working words; e.g., VIABLE is a working word to apply to a newly formed organism, though nothing if not stylish when used to indicate that a political programme is practicable; *initiate* is a working word for formal admission to an office or society though stylish as a mere synonym for *begin;* DEEM is a working word in the sense in which lawyers use it, though stylish for *think.* Others again, such as *bodeful* and *dwell* and *perchance,* lose their unhappy stylish air when they are in surroundings of their own kind, where they are not conspicuous like an escaped canary among the sparrows.

What is to be deprecated is the notion that one can improve one's style by using stylish words, or that important occasions necessarily demand important words. The motorist before the magistrate does not improve his chances of acquittal by saying *I observed that I should not impede her progress* when he means *I saw that I should not get in her way.*

# Interludes

# 4

E. B. White remembers the man who taught him to write, and Katherine Anne Porter looks back over her life as a writer to attempt to define her attitude toward style. In further *Paris Review* interviews like the one with Miss Porter, Marianne Moore, Georges Simenon, Mary McCarthy, and Truman Capote respond to questions on the same subject.

# E. B. WHITE

"OMIT needless words!" cries the author on page 21, and into that imperative Will Strunk really put his heart and soul. In the days when I was sitting in his class, he omitted so many needless words, and omitted them so forcibly and with such eagerness and obvious relish, that he often seemed in the position of having short-changed himself, a man left with nothing more to say yet with time to fill, a radio prophet who had outdistanced the clock. Will Strunk got out of this predicament by a simple trick: he uttered every sentence three times. When he delivered his oration on brevity to the class, he leaned forward over his desk, grasped his coat lapels in his hands, and in a husky, conspiratorial voice said, "Rule Thirteen. Omit needless words! Omit needless words! Omit needless words!"

He was a memorable man, friendly and funny. Under the remembered sting of his kindly lash, I have been trying to omit needless words since 1919, and although there are still many words that cry for omission and the huge task will never be accomplished, it is exciting to me to reread

[E. B. White is writing about his old English teacher, Will Strunk, and about Strunk's book on prose style. This excerpt, without postscript, originally appeared in *The New Yorker*, copyright © 1957 by E. B. White, and in the Introduction to *The Elements of Style* by William Strunk, Jr. and E. B. White (Macmillan, 1959). "Postscript," copyright © 1962 by E. B. White, and "Will Strunk" appeared in *The Points of My Compass* by E. B. White (Harper & Row, 1962). Reprinted by permission.]

the masterly Strunkian elaboration of this noble theme. It goes:

> Vigorous writing is concise. A sentence should contain no unnecessary words, a paragraph no unnecessary sentences, for the same reason that a drawing should have no unnecessary lines and a machine no unnecessary parts. This requires not that the writer make all his sentences short, or that he avoid all detail and treat his subjects only in outline, but that every word tell.

There you have a short, valuable essay on the nature and beauty of brevity—sixty-three words that could change the world. Having recovered from his adventure in prolixity (sixty-three words were a lot of words in the tight world of William Strunk, Jr.), the Professor proceeds to give a few quick lessons in pruning. The student learns to cut the deadwood from "This is a subject which . . . ," reducing it to "This subject . . . ," a gain of three words. He learns to trim ". . . used for fuel purposes" down to "used for fuel." He learns that he is being a chatterbox when he says "The question as to whether" and that he should just say "Whether"—a gain of four words out of a possible five.

The Professor devotes a special paragraph to the vile expression "the fact that," a phrase that causes him to quiver with revulsion. The expression, he says, should be "revised out of every sentence in which it occurs." But a shadow of gloom seems to hang over the page, and you feel that he knows how hopeless his cause is. I suppose I have written "the fact that" a thousand times in the heat of composition, revised it out maybe five hundred times in the cool aftermath. To be batting only .500 this late in the season, to fail half the time to connect with this fat pitch, saddens me, for it seems a betrayal of the man who showed me how to swing at it and made the swinging seem worth while.

\*
\*
\*

It was during the permissive years that the third edition of Webster's *New International Dictionary* was being put together, along new lines of lexicography, and it was Dr.

Gove, the head man, who perhaps expressed the whole thing most succinctly when he remarked that a dictionary "should have no traffic with . . . artificial notions of correctness or superiority. It must be descriptive and not prescriptive." This approach struck many people as chaotic and degenerative, and that's the way it strikes me. Strunk was a fundamentalist; he believed in right and wrong, and so, in the main, do I. Unless someone is willing to entertain notions of superiority, the English language disintegrates, just as a home disintegrates unless someone in the family sets standards of good taste, good conduct, and simple justice.

# KATHERINE ANNE PORTER

INTERVIEWER: You are frequently spoken of as a stylist. Do you think a style can be cultivated, or at least refined?

Porter: I've been called a stylist until I really could tear my hair out. And I simply don't believe in style. The style is you. Oh, you can cultivate a style, I suppose, if you like. But I should say it remains a cultivated style. It remains artificial and imposed, and I don't think it deceives anyone. A cultivated style would be like a mask. Everybody knows it's a mask, and sooner or later you must show yourself— or at least, you show yourself as someone who could not afford to show himself, and so created something to hide behind. Style is the man. Aristotle said it first, as far as I know, and everybody has said it since, because it is one of those unarguable truths. You do not create a style. You work, and develop yourself; your style is an emanation from your own being.

\*
\*
\*

[The interview with Miss Porter, and the interviews that follow, were published originally in The Paris Review and collected in two volumes called Writers at Work. From Writers at Work: The Paris Review Interviews, First Series, edited by Malcolm Cowley. Copyright © 1957, 1958 by The Paris Review, Inc. And from Writers at Work: The Paris Review Interviews, Second Series. Copyright © 1963 by The Paris Review, Inc. Reprinted by permission of The Viking Press, Inc. and Martin Secker and Warbury Ltd.]

. . . , I mastered my craft as well as I could. There is a technique, there is a craft, and you have to learn it. Well, I did as well as I could with that, but now all in the world I am interested in is telling a story. I have something to tell you that I, for some reason, think is worth telling, and so I want to tell it as clearly and purely and simply as I can. But I had spent fifteen years at least learning to write. I practiced writing in every possible way that I could. I wrote a pastiche of other people, imitating Dr. Johnson and Laurence Sterne, and Petrarch and Shakespeare's sonnets, and then I tried writing my own way. I spent fifteen years learning to trust myself; that's what it comes to. Just as a pianist runs his scales for ten years before he gives his concert: because when he gives that concert, he can't be thinking of his fingering or of his hands; he has to be thinking of his interpretation, of the music he's playing. He's thinking of what he's trying to communicate. And if he hasn't got his technique perfected by then, he needn't give the concert at all.

\*
\*
\*

Porter: I love the purity of language. I keep cautioning my students and anyone who will listen to me not to use the jargon of trades, not to use scientific language, because they're going to be out of date the day after tomorrow. The scientists change their vocabulary, their jargon, every day. So do the doctors, and the politicians, and the theologians—every body, every profession, every trade changes its vocabulary all of the time. But there is a basic pure human speech that exists in every language. And that is the language of the poet and the writer. So many words that had good meanings once upon a time have come to have meanings almost evil—certainly inaccurate. And "psychology" is one of them. It has been so abused. This awful way a whole segment, not a generation but too many of the young writers, have got so soaked in the Freudian and post-Freudian vocabulary that they can't speak—not only can't speak English, but they can't speak *any* human language anymore. You can't write about people out of text-

122

books, and you can't use a jargon. You have to speak clearly and simply and purely in a language that a six-year-old child can understand; and yet have the meanings and the overtones of language, and the implications, that appeal to the highest intelligence—that is, the highest intelligence that one is able to reach.

# MARIANNE MOORE

INTERVIEWER: I wanted to ask you a few questions about poetry in general. Somewhere you have said that originality is a by-product of sincerity. You often use moral terms in your criticism. Is the necessary morality specifically literary, a moral use of words, or is it larger? In what way must a man be good if he is to write good poems?

Moore: If emotion is strong enough, the words are unambiguous. Someone asked Robert Frost (is this right?) if he was selective. He said, "Call it passionate preference." Must a man be good to write good poems? The villains in Shakespeare are not illiterate, are they? But rectitude *has* a ring that is implicative, I would say. And with *no* integrity, a man is not likely to write the kind of book I read.

# GEORGES SIMENON

SIMENON: Just one piece of general advice from a writer has been very useful to me. It was from Colette. I was writing short stories for *Le Matin,* and Colette was literary editor at that time. I remember I gave her two short stories and she returned them and I tried again and tried again. Finally she said, "Look, it is too literary, always too literary." So I followed her advice. It's what I do when I write, the main job when I rewrite.

Interviewer: What do you mean by "too literary"? What do you cut out, certain kinds of words?

Simenon: Adjectives, adverbs, and every word which is there just to make an effect. Every sentence which is there just for the sentence. You know, you have a beautiful sentence—cut it. Every time I find such a thing in one of my novels it is to be cut.

# MARY McCARTHY

. . . *Whatever* way I write was really, I suppose, formed critically. That is, I learned to write reviews and criticism and then write novels so that however I wrote, it was formed that way. George Eliot, you know, began by translating Strauss, began by writing about German philosophy —though her philosophic passages are not at all good in *Middlemarch*. Neverthless, I *think* that this kind of training really makes one more interested in the subject than in the style. Her work certainly doesn't suffer from any kind of stylistic frippery. There's certainly no voluminous drapery around. There is a kind of concision in it, at her best—that passage where she's describing the character of Lydgate—which shows, I think, the critical and philosophic training. I've never liked the conventional conception of "style." What's confusing is that style usually means some form of fancy writing—when people say, oh yes, so and so's such a "wonderful stylist." But if one means by style the voice, the irreducible and always recognizable and alive thing, then of course style is really everything.

# TRUMAN CAPOTE

INTERVIEWER: You seem to make a distinction between writers who are stylists and writers who aren't. Which writers would you call stylists and which not?

Capote: What is style? And "what" as the Zen Koan asks, "is the sound of one hand [clapping]?" No one really *knows*; yet either you *know* or you don't. For myself, if

124

you will excuse a rather cheap little image, I suppose style is the mirror of an artist's sensibility—more so than the *content* of his work. To some degree all writers have style— Ronald Firbank, bless his heart, had little else, and thank God he realized it. But the possession of style, *a* style, is often a hindrance, a negative force, not as it should be, and as it is—with, say E. M. Forster and Colette and Flaubert and Mark Twain and Hemingway and Isak Dinesen—a reinforcement. Dreiser, for instance, has *a* style—but oh, *Dio buono!* And Eugene O'Neill. And Faulkner, brilliant as he is. They all seem to me triumphs over strong but negative styles, styles that do not really add to the communication between writer and reader. Then there is the styleless stylist—which is very difficult, very admirable, and *always* very popular: Graham Greene, Maugham, Thornton Wilder, John Hersey, Willa Cather, Thurber, Sartre (remember, we're *not* discussing content), J. P. Marquand, and so on. But yes, there *is* such an animal as a nonstylist. Only they're not writers; they're typists. Sweaty typists blacking up pounds of bond paper with formless, eyeless, earless messages. Well, who are some of the younger writers who seem to know that style exists? P. H. Newby, Françoise Sagan, somewhat. Bill Styron, Flannery O'Connor—she has some fine moments, that girl. James Merrill. William Goyen—if he'd stop being hysterical. J. D. Salinger —especially in the colloquial tradition. Colin Wilson? Another typist.

# H. L. Mencken

## EUPHEMISMS

The American seldom believes that the trade he follows
is quite worthy of his virtues and talents; he thinks that
he would have adorned something far gaudier. Since it is
often impossible for him to escape, or to dream plausibly
of escaping, he soothes himself by pretending that he
belongs to a superior section of his craft, and even invents
a sonorous name to set himself off from the herd. Here
we glimpse the origin of characteristic American euphemisms, e.g., *mortician* for *undertaker, realtor* for *real-estate
agent, beautician* for *hairdresser, exterminating engineer*
for *rat catcher* and so on. *Realtor* was devised by a high-
toned real-estate agent of Minneapolis, Charles N. Chad-
bourn by name, who sought a distinctive title by which he
and his fellow members of the Minneapolis Real Estate
Board could distinguish themselves from fly-by-night dealers in houses and lots. The Minneapolis brethren were so
pleased with their new name that he went to the conven-
tion of the National Association of Real Estate Boards at
New Orleans, and made a formal offer of it, which was
accepted gratefully. The general counsel of the National
Association is heard from every time *realtor* is taken in
vain, and when, in 1922, Sinclair Lewis applied it to
George F. Babbitt, there was an uproar. But when Mr. Chad-
bourn was appealed to he decided that Babbitt was "fairly
well described," for he was "a prominent member of the

[From *The American Language* by H. L. Mencken. Copyright
1919 by Alfred A. Knopf, Inc. and renewed 1947 by H. L.
Mencken. Reprinted by permission of the publisher.]

local board and of the State association," and one could scarcely look for anything better in "a book written in the ironic vein of the author of 'Main Street.'"

The suggestion that *realtor* is derived from two Spanish words, *real*, meaning royal, and *toro*, bull, and that it thus connotes *royal bull*, is spurned by the bearers of the name. The official pronunciation is not re*a*ltor, but *reel*tor. The agent suffix *-or* has always conveyed a more dignified suggestion in English than the allied *-er*, perhaps because it often represents the Latin *-ator* or the French *-eur*. Professor, to most persons, is superior to *teacher* not only in meaning but also in aspect and atmosphere, and in the same way *author* stands above *writer*, and (at least in his own eyes) an *advisor* to students is more dignified than a mere *adviser*. In this great free Republic there is little hostility to human aspiration, and in consequence *realtor* has suggested insuror (an insurance agent), *furnitor* (a furniture dealer), *publicator* (a press agent) and *weldor*. The radio trade has a long list of terms in *-or*, but they are applied to mechanical contrivances, not to God's children, *e.g.*, *resistor, inductor, capacitator* and *arrestor*, the last an elegant substitute for the earlier *lightning arrester*, which is traced by the DAE to 1860 and is probably an Americanism.

*Mortician* is in the public domain. It was suggested by *physician*, for undertakers naturally admire and like to pal with the resurrection men. From the earliest days they have sought to bedizen their hocus-pocus with mellifluous euphemisms, and during the Civil War they undertook their first really radical reform of its terms, by substituting *casket* for the older *coffin*. Many purists did not like it, including Nathaniel Hawthorne, who thus denounced it in "Our Old Home" (1863):

> *Caskets!*—a vile modern phrase [*sic*] which compels a person of sense and good taste to shrink more disgustfully than ever before from the idea of being buried at all.

But *casket* quickly made its way, and since the early 80s *coffin* has seldom appeared in an American undertaker's advertisement or in a newspaper account of the funeral of anyone above the dignity of an executed murderer. *Casket* remains in almost universal use, though there are poetic morticians who root for *slumber cot* or *burial couch*. The Civil War also brought the embalming of the dead into common practice, thanks to the job of bringing home dead soldiers from distant battlefields, often in warm weather. All the pioneer embalmers of the time called themselves *Dr.*

The DAE's earliest example of *mortician* comes from an advertisement in the Columbus (Ohio) *Dispatch* of August 14, 1895, only six months after the term was launched by the *Embalmer's Monthly*. But it was not until September 17, 1917, that 200 of the most eminent American undertakers banded themselves into an organization called the National Selected *Morticians*, and began to strike out for a general reform of necrophoric nomenclature. Some of their inventions are now familiar: *patient* or *case* for *body; funeral car, casket coach* or *ambulance* for *hearse; negligee, slumber robe* or *slumber shirt* for *shroud; slumber room, reposing room, funeral home* or *funeral residence* for *funeral parlor* or *undertaking establishment; operating parlor, operating room, preparing room* or *preparation room* for the cellar in which the embalmer does his work; *service car* for *dead wagon; limousine* for *mourners' coach;* and so on. In September 1935, a Washington mortician was advertising by cards in the local trolley cars that the *reposing rooms* in his *funeral home* were "*autumn-breezed* by the finest air-conditioning equipment." Meanwhile, the owners and press agents of places of sepulcher have followed their associates into the flowery fields of euphemism. Graveyards, in all the more progressive parts of the United States, are graveyards no longer, nor even cemeteries, but *memorial parks, burial abbeys* or *-cloisters,* or *mortaria.* In some areas graveyards are giving way to elaborate buildings. Some of these new mausoleums are structures of great pretentiousness, usually either Gothic or Byzantine in style and as gorgeous as a first-rate filling station. They flourish especially in southern California, and those of Los Angeles are heavily patronized, for one of the inducements they offer is the chance to store the beloved dead check by jowl with a Clark Gable or a Marilyn Monroe. To be laid away in one runs into money. Even a run-of-the-mine funeral costs over $1,000, and in a year the morticians and their satellites extract three times as much money from American pockets as is spent on doctors, hospitals and prescription drugs. Some of these virtuosi are folk of literary genius, as the *Charon Equipment Company*, of Chicago, which rents funeral appurtenances, or the Cooney Mortuary, of the same city, which describes itself as "A Homey Place for Funerals."

A correspondent reported a *mortician* in the town of Driffield in Yorkshire (pop. 6,000) in 1925, but the term has made very little progress among the hunkerous English, who prefer *undertaker*. *Funeral director*, an Americanism traced to 1886, is not listed in the OED, but an older term, *funeral undertaker*, is traced to 1707. *Undertaker* itself goes back to 1698. *Morgue*, to designate a dead house, was borrowed from the French in 1850, and *mortuary* dates from 1865. *Crematory* is traced by the DAE in American use to 1885; the OED traces it to 1876 in England. It is now pretty well supplanted in the United States by the more mellifluous *crematorium*, which borrows elegance from *pastorium*, *lubritorium* and their congeners.

The resounding success of *mortician* brought in many other words in *-ician*, e.g., *beautician*, *cosmetician*, *radiotrician*, *linguistician*. The DA's first citation of *beautician* is dated 1926, but the owner of a beauty salon by the name of Miss Kathryn Ann was advertising in the November 1924 issue of the Cleveland, Ohio, telephone directory that she had a staff of "very efficient *beauticians*." By 1926 Dr. Morris Fishbein, editor of the *Journal of the American Medical Association*, was reporting in the *American Mercury* that *beauticians*, *cosmeticians* and *cosmetologists* were in practice from end to end of the country, and that nine states had already passed acts providing for their examination, licensing and regulation.

*Beautician* had reached England by 1937, but it was apparently collared there by beauty-preparation manufacturers, who also tried to lay hands on *cosmetician*. In the United States both are yielding to *cosmetologist*, and the chief organization of the beauty-shop operators is called the National Hairdressers and *Cosmetologists* Association. In the Nineteenth Century the dens of lady hairdressers were called simply *hairdressing* parlors, but *beauty parlor* began to appear before World War I, and soon afterward it was displaced by *beauty shop, beauty shoppe* and *beauty salon.*

*Radiotrician*, perhaps suggested by *electrician* rather than by *mortician*, was adopted by the radio repairmen in the late 1920s, a little while after the regular electrical jobbers began to call themselves *electragists;* both terms now have little currency among the laity. *Shoetrician* is likewise uncommon; however, the earlier euphemism *shoe rebuilder* flourishes, and some brethren of the craft are still content to be *cobblers. Fizzician*, a second stage (the first being *fountaineer*) in the advance from *soda jerk*, was reported by *PM* in 1938. *Linguistician* has been proposed to distinguish the scientific students of language from mere polyglots—which is what the term *linguist* usually signifies to the hoi polloi—but the resemblance to *mortician* has repelled the sensitive-eared members of the profession. *American Speech* has recorded such marvels as *whooptician, fermentician, bootblackitician* and *scholastician. Ecstatician* ("one who studies, or is versed in, ecstasies") turned up in the *Atlantic Monthly* in 1936, and *jazzician* briefly in England in 1938. *Bootician*, my own invention, launched in the *American Mercury* in 1925, to designate a high-toned bootlegger, was followed in 1930 by *super-bootician*. It came too late to be included in the DAE or DA.

The tendency to engaud lowly vocations with names presumably dignified goes back to the Revolution, and has been frequently noted by English travelers, beginning with Thomas Anburey in 1779. In 1784 John Ferdinand Dalziel Smyth observed that the smallest American shopkeepers were calling their establishments *stores*, which indicated a large place to an Englishman. "The different distinct branches of manufacturers," he said, "such as *hosiers, haberdashers, clothiers, linen drapers, grocers, stationers,* etc., are not known here; they are all comprehended in the single name and occupation of *merchant* or *storekeeper.*" By 1846 the American barbershop had begun to be a *shaving salon,* and by 1850 a photographer was a *daguerrian artist.* By 1875 barbers were *tonsorial artists* or *tonsorialists,* and in the early 80s presentable saloonkeepers became *restauranters* or *restauranteurs.* By 1901 the *Police Gazette* was carrying on a campaign for the abandonment of the lowly *bartender* and the adoption of either *bar clerk* or *mixologist,* which last had been proposed sportively by the *Knickerbocker Magazine* in 1856 and had come into more or less use in the West by 1870. The early American photographers called their working places *studios,* and the term was later adopted by the operators of billiard rooms, barbershops and even various sorts of stores. A contributor to *American Speech,* in 1926, reported encountering *tonsorial studio, food studio* and *shoe studio.* In 1940 the makers of Fanny Farmer candies called their kitchens *studios,* as did a Canadian competitor.

The list of such euphemisms might be lengthened almost endlessly. A bill collector has described himself as a *collection correspondent,* a tape-worm specialist has operated a *Helminthological Institute,* and in some stores *section manager* (formerly *aisle manager*) has replaced *floor walker. Tree surgeon* appears in Webster 1961 without comment; in 1934 the man who coined it, Martin L. Davey, was elected governor of Ohio. *Corn doctors* have progressed via *chiropodists* to *podiatrists.* The old-time newsboy is now a *newspaper boy,* which seems to be regarded as somehow more dignified; a dog catcher is a *canine control officer* in Peoria, Ill., and a *humane officer* in Tulsa, Okla.; an iceman, in Denver, is an *ice attendant;* a grocer is a *provisioner* or *victualer.* A janitor is a *superintendent, custodian, engineer-custodian* or *custodial engineer.* At some universities, when the janitors were elevated to *custodians*, the custodians of special library collections were in turn upgraded to *directors* or *archivists*. In 1940 the International Brotherhood of *Red Caps* changed its name to the United *Transport Service Employees* of America. In 1939, when the surviving customers' men in the offices of the New York stockbrokers formed an Association of *Customers' Men* there was diffidence about their title, which had suffered grievously from the town wits; they soon adopted *customers' broker*. Three years before this the hod carriers of Milwaukee had resolved to be *mason laborers,* and only a few months later the Long Island Federation of Women's Clubs decreed that housewives should become *homemakers*. In 1942 some reformer in Kansas City launched a crusade to make it *household executive*. In 1943 the more solvent spiritualists of the country, fretting under the discreditable connotations of their name, resolved to be *psychists* thenceforth.

Gardeners posturing as *landscape architects* and laborers posturing as *gardeners* are too numerous to be remarked. So are lobbyists under the guise of *industrial consultants* or *field engineers*, press agents disguised as *publicity directors, public relations counsel* or *publicists*, detectives as *investigators* or *operatives*, encyclopedia salesmen as *educational advisors* and messenger boys as *communications carriers*. *Public relations counsel* was launched by Edward L. Bernays, of New York, one of the most distinguished members of the fraternity.

The lowly garbageman and ashman (English: *dustman*) have begun to disappear from the American fauna; they are now becoming *sanitary officers,* and the bureau under which the former works (at all events in heavenly Pasadena) has become the *table waste disposal department*. In refreshingly conservative contrast, Chicago still has *public scavengers*. Street sweeps are also becoming *sanitary officers* or *sanitation men*. The United States Post Office now calls its male sweepers *charmen*, and may be trusted on some near tomorrow to give a lift to its *charwomen*. The junkmen, by their own resolve, are now *waste material dealers*. An ancient bill sticker attached to a Baltimore theater once boasted the sonorous title of *chief lithographer*.

Before the Revolution *help* and *hired man* seem to have been descriptive merely; Albert Matthews maintains with his accustomed great learning that before 1776 there was not "the slightest indication of *hired man* having been employed in a euphemistic sense." But after 1776 it began to be employed to distinguish a freeman from a slave, and after 1863 it became a general substitute for *servant*, a "hated appellation." It was not noted as an Americanism by any of the early writers on the subject, but Webster listed it in his American Dictionary of 1828. *Hired girl* is traced to 1818, *hired hand* to the same year and *hired help* to 1815. *Help* originally appears to have designated a person giving occasional assistance only, as opposed to a regular servant. It probably became a euphemism after the Revolution, when the servant problem became acute. *Help* and *hired girl* are now both abandoned, and *maid* or *housekeeper* is the almost universal designation of a female servant.

Since *engineer* became a title of prestige in America, it has been assumed by a wide spectrum of charlatans. For a number of years the *Engineering News-Record*, the organ of the legitimate engineers, used to devote a column every week to uninvited invaders of the craft, some so fantastic that it was constrained to reproduce their business cards photographically to convince its readers that it was not spoofing. A favorite exhibit was a bedding manufacturer who first became a *mattress engineer* and then promoted himself to the lofty dignity of *sleep engineer*. No doubt he would have called himself a *morphician* if he had thought of it. A tractor driver advertised for a job as a *caterpillar engineer*. A beautician burst out as an *appearance engineer*. Elsewhere appeared *display engineers* who had been lowly window dressers until some visionary among them made the great leap, *demolition engineers* who were once content to be house wreckers and *sanitary engineers* who had an earlier incarnation as garbagemen. The *wedding engineer* is a technician employed by florists to dress churches for hymeneal orgies. The *commence-ment engineer* arranges college and high-school commencements; he has lists of clergymen who may be trusted to pray briefly, and some sort of fire-alarm connection with popular commencement orators. The *packing engineer* crates clocks, radios and chinaware for shipment. The *correspondence engineer* writes selling letters guaranteed to pull. The *income engineer* is an insurance solicitor in a new false face. The *dwelling engineer* replaces lost keys, repairs leaky roofs and plugs up rat holes in the cellar. The *vision engineer* supplies spectacles at cut rates. The *de-horning engineer* attends to bulls who grow too frisky. Perhaps the prize should go to the *dansant engineer* (an agent supplying dancers and musicians to night clubs), or to the *hot-dog engineer*.

The Dictionary of Occupational Titles prepared by the Job Analysis and Information Section of the Division of Standards and Research of the Department of Labor lists many curious varieties of engineers, including the *rigging-up engineer*, the *yarder engineer* and the *roader engineer*, but all of them appear to have to do with some form of actual engineering or engine operation, however lowly, and so their titles, while perhaps rather florid, do not qualify as euphemisms. In this list a *sanitary engineer* appears, not as a plumber but as "a civil engineer who designs and supervises the construction and operation of sewers, sewage disposal plants, garbage disposal plants, ventilation tunnels, and other sanitary facilities," and such savants as the *termite engineer*, the *social engineer* and the *human engineer* are *non est*. Neither do any of these latter-day wizards appear on the list of engineers employed by the Tennessee Valley Authority, though it has room for *cost engineers*, *erosion engineers* and *material engineers*. The rat, cockroach and bedbug eradicators of the country have had for years an organization called the American Society of *Exterminating Engineers*. On November 8, 1923, the *News-Record* reported that one of its members followed the sideline of a mortician in Bristol, Pa., and suggested sportively: "That's service for you. Kill 'em and bury 'em for the same fee." But the title of *engineer* seems to be reserved with some plausibility for the head men of this profession: its lowlier representatives are apparently content to call themselves *exterminators*.

Next to *engineer*, *expert* seems to be the favorite talisman of Americans eager to augment their estate and dignity in this world. Very often it is hitched to an explanatory prefix, e.g., *housing-*, *hog-*, *marketing-* or *sheep-dip-*, but sometimes the simple adjective *trained-* suffices. When the Brain Trust was in power in Washington, the town swarmed with such quacks. A humorous member of Congress found at least one whose expertness was acquired in a seminary for chiropractors. During the John Purroy Mitchel "reform" administration in New York City (1914-18) so many bogus *experts* were put on the payroll that special designations ran out, and a number were carried as *general experts*.

After the invention of *bootician* in 1925 I hatched no neologism of the same high tone for fifteen years. Then I was inspired by a letter from a lady subscribing herself Georgia Southern and designating her profession as strip teasing, who requested "a new and more palatable word to describe this art." As a help to her (or her public relations counsel) I replied as follows:

> It might be a good idea to relate strip teasing in some way or other to the associated zoological phenomenon of molting. Thus the word *moltician* comes to mind, but it must be rejected because of its likeness to *mortician*.
>
> A resort to the scientific name for molting, which is *ecdysis*, produces both *ecdysist* and *ecdysiast*. Then there are suggestions in the names of some of the creatures which practice molting. The scientific name for the common crab is *Callinectes hastatus*, which produces *callinectian*. Again there is a family of lizards called the *Geckonidae*, and their name produces *gecko*.

In a little while articles in the public prints indicated that she (or her press agent) had decided to adopt *ecdysiast*. It appeared by these articles that two popularizers of semantics had been consulted—S. I. Hayakawa, of the Illinois

Institute of Technology and author of "Language in Action," and Stuart Chase, S.B. *cum laude* (Harvard), author of "The Economy of Abundance," "Your Money's Worth," "The Tyranny of Words," and other scientific works. Hayakawa seemingly demurred on the incredible ground that he had never seen a strip teaser in action, and Chase, busy with the salvation of humanity on a dozen fronts, made no reply at all; so I won by a sort of forfeit. Soon the British United Press correspondent cabled news of *ecdysiast* to London, and it was discussed gravely in many of the great English organs of opinion, though strip teasing itself was prohibited in the British Isles. A suggestion by La Sothern (or her press agent) to the official censor of stage performances that the adoption of *ecdysiast* might perchance open the way for lifting the ban regrettably got nowhere. But the inevitable Association of *Ecdysiast*s soon appeared in the United States. Rather curiously, the most eminent of all the ecdysiasts, Gypsy Rose Lee, refused to adopt the new name.

Englishmen are a good deal less ashamed of their trades than Americans, and in consequence show less exuberance of occupational euphemism. But as long ago as the Seventeenth Century some of the more advanced English dressers of female coiffures called themselves *woman surgeons*, and before the end of that century some English men's tailors claimed to be *master fashioners*. Today many of the buyers and sellers of old clothes in London pass as *wardrobe dealers*, and from time to time there are proposals to outfit street sweeps with some more delicate name. In 1944 the charwomen working in the government offices in London were organized into the Government Minor and Manipulative Grades Association of *Office Cleaners*, and the Glasgow *dustmen* (American: garbagemen) were renamed *cleansing personnel*. Meanwhile, the rat-catching department of the Ministry of Food had become the *directorate of infestation control*, and the rat-catcher became a *rodent operative*. Many English butchers already call themselves *purveyors*, usually in the form of *purveyors of quality*, and those of Birmingham use *meat traders*, and have set up a *Meat-Traders'* Diploma Society which issues diplomas to its members, and calls its meat cutters *meat salesmen*, just as American milk-wagon drivers are called *milk salesmen* and bakers' deliverymen *bread salesmen*. The fishmongers still vacillate between *fish specialist* and *seafood caterer*, the latter borrowed from America. The English used-car dealers and other such idealists are also showing signs of unrest, for P. E. Cleator encountered a *car clinic* at Wrexham, in North Wales, in 1937. Finally, *Punch* reports that a Cheshire cobbler, disdaining both *shoe rebuilder* and *shoetrician*, calls himself a *practipedist*.

The English euphemism-of-all-work used to be *lady*. In the Seventeenth Century the court poet Edmund Waller spoke of actresses, then a novelty on the English stage, as *lady actors*, and even today the English newspapers frequently refer to *lady secretaries*, *lady doctors*, *lady inspectors* and *lady champions*. *Women's wear*, in most English shops, is *ladies' wear*. But this excessive use of *lady* seems to be going out, and *women's singles* and *women's ice hockey* are seen on the sports pages of the London *Daily Telegraph*. In the United States *lady* is more definitely out of favor. The *salesladies* of yesteryear are now *saleswomen* or *salesgirls*, and the female superintendent of a hospital is simply the *superintendent*. The DA traces *saleslady* to 1856 and *forelady* to 1889. Now and then a new congener appears, *e.g.*, *flag lady*, which the Union Pacific Railroad introduced in 1944 to designate female watchers at grade crossings. But the women at work in the shipyards and other war plants were seldom if ever called *ladies* and the Pennsylvania Railroad, when it put female trainmen to work in 1943, marked their caps simply *trainman*. When women were first elected to Congress, the leaders of the House of Representatives used "the *lady* from So-and-so," but soon "the *gentlewoman*" was substituted. Its invention is commonly ascribed to Nicholas Longworth, son-in-law of Theodore Roosevelt. He probably suggested it jocosely, for it is clumsy and often as inaccurate as *lady*. The English normally use just the *hon. member* for women M.P.'s, though sometimes the *hon. lady* occurs. The English use *gentleman* much more carefully than we do, and much more carefully than they themselves use *lady*. *Gentleman author* or *gentleman clerk* would make them howl, but they commonly employ *gentleman rider* and *gentleman player* in place of our *amateur*, though *amateur* seems to be gaining favor. Here the man referred to is always actually a gentleman by their standards. What with World War II and the welfare state, the English use of *lady* has gone into a decline. But it survives as a form of address hooked to *Lord* and *Sir*, as well as in *lady mayoress*. On May 7, 1937, the New York *Herald Tribune* printed a London dispatch saying that "the retiring rooms specially erected at Westminster Abbey for Coronation Day will be severally marked as follows: *Peers, Gentlemen, Men,* and *Peeresses, Ladies, Women,*" but this seems to have been a rather unusual reversion to ancient forms. On the signs in the public lavatories of London *ladies* and *women* appear to be varied without rule, the *ladies* and *men* may grace adjacent doors. The English still cling to the suffix *-ess,* and use it much oftener than Americans. Such of these common forms as *mayoress* or *manageress* would strike most Americans as very odd, and so would *conductress* (of a streetcar). But the older forms in *-ess* are still alive in the United States, *e.g., deaconess, patroness* and *poetess.* During the era of elegance straddling the Civil War the termination was considered rather swagger, and some grotesque examples came into use. Mamie Meredith has assembled *doctress, lecturess, nabobess, rebeless, traderess, astronomess, editress* and *mulatress;* the comic writers of the time contributed *championess, Mormoness* and *prestidigitateuress.* The OED traces *sculptress,* in English use, to 1662, and the DAE traces *presidentess,* in English use, to 1782, and, in American use, to 1819. James Fenimore Cooper used *Americaness* in his "Home as Found" (1838). But it never caught on.

Euphemisms for things are almost as common in the United States as euphemisms for avocations. Dozens of forlorn little fresh-water colleges are called *universities,* and almost all *pawnshops* are *loan offices*. *City*, in England, used to be confined to the seats of bishops, and even today it is applied only to considerable places, but in the United States it is commonly assumed by any town with paved streets, and in the statistical publications of the federal government it is applied to all places of 8,000 or more population. In Louisiana, hamlets of 450 population proudly advertise *city limits;* in Alaska, a first-class city needs only 400 inhabitants, and a second-class city a scant 50.

Meanwhile, such harsh terms as *secondhand* and *ready-made* disappear from the American vocabulary. For the former, automobile dealers, who are ardent euphemists, have substituted *reconditioned, rebuilt, repossessed* and *used;* and for the latter, department stores offer *ready-tailored, ready-to-wear* and *ready-to-put-on*. Los Angeles reported *experienced tires* during the early days of World War II rationing. In New York a secondhand store is now often called a *buy-and-sell shop;* in Chicago it may also be a *resale store* or a *resale shop*. There is also a continuous flow of euphemisms for *damaged* or *shop-worn, e.g., second, slightly second, slightly hurt, store-used* and *substandard*. The last had got to England by 1938. In 1942 the *ersatz* articles introduced with rationing and priorities brought a demand for a word less offensive to the refined mind than *substitute*. In the canning industry materials used as substitutes for tin were called *alternates*. The appearance of horse meat for human consumption in 1943 started a search for euphemisms to designate it. One reader of *Life* submitted a list of names for dishes designated "to tempt the most ticklish palates," including *braised fetlocks* and *fillet of Pegasus*. But sometimes, in revulsion against euphemism, a bold advertiser tells the truth. Thus, from a correspondent in California comes a clipping of an advertisement of a Carmel restaurant, announcing *pseudo mint juleps,* and a Baltimore department store has advertised *fake pearls*.

The uplifters are naturally heavy users of ameliorative and disarming words. One of the best of recent coinage

is *door-key children,* a humane designation for the young-
sters who are turned loose on the city streets to shift for
themselves. In the lunatic asylums (now *state hospitals* or
*mental hospitals* or *psychiatric institutes*) a guard is an
*attendant,* a violent patient is *assaultive* and one whose
aberration is not all-out is *maladjusted.* In the federal
prisons a guard is a *custodial officer;* among social workers
*case work* has become *personal service,* and every surviving orphan asylum has become an *infant home* or something equally mellifluous. In many American cities what
used to be the office of the overseers of the poor is now
the *community welfare department.* The English, in this
field of gilding the unpleasant facts of life, yield nothing
to Americans. Their reform schools for wayward boys,
which had been *Borstal institutions* since 1902, are now
called *approved schools,* and there is talk of further
change to *hostels. Slum clearance* still appeals to the British politician; *a special area,* formerly *a depressed area,*
designates an industrially or economically depressed part
of the country with heavy unemployment. In the United
States *slum clearance* has largely given way to *urban re-
newal.*

The early moviehouses were called *parlors,* but in a
little while *theaters* was substituted, and today *theater*
ordinarily suggests movies to an American. The first *movie
cathedral* to bedazzle the fans was the Paramount Theatre
in New York. Unhappily, the newspaper wits began to
poke fun at it by writing about *movie mosques, movie
synagogues* and *movie filling stations,* and so it did not
prosper. But as late as 1941 a *news cathedral* was opened
in Poughkeepsie, N.Y., and in Pittsburgh the huge sky-
scraper housing the town university is called the *Cathedral
of Learning.* For many years there has been a quiet effort
to find a substitute for *mother-in-law,* which has been
cursed with unpleasant connotations by the cheaper humor
of the press and stage, and also, perhaps, by personal experience. Gene Howe, editor of the Amarillo (Tex.) *News-
Globe,* a son of the cynical E. W. Howe, but himself a man
of heart, began a movement for rehabilitating the lady in

1930, or thereabout, but did not invent a softer name. In 1942, however, the Mother-in-Law Association that flowed from his campaign adopted *kin-mother*, which had been proposed by Mrs. E. M. Sullivan. Other suggestions were *our-ma, law-ma, assistant mother, ersatz mother* and *moth-erette*. But *kin-mother* won.

Substitutes for *death* and *to die*, both euphemistic and facetious, have been numerous in America since the earliest days. Many of the latter class are heritages from England, *e.g., to croak, to kick the bucket* and *to peg out*, but others are of American origin, *e.g., to pass in one's checks, to go under* (traced by the DAE to 1848) and the short form *to kick. To go West* may be American also, though the DAE does not list it and it was used by the British soldiers in World War I. The same may be said with more certainty of *to blow off; to bite the dust, to fold, to hop off, to lose the decision, to pass out, to poop out, to shuffle off* and *to shoot the works*. Similarly, for *death* there are *the one-way ticket, the fade-out, the last call* and *the payoff,* and for *dead, checked out, finished gone under* and *washed up.* In the days of Prohibition the racketeers invented (or had invented for them by newspaper reporters) a number of picturesque terms for *to kill, e.g., to take for a ride, to put on the spot, to put the finger on* and *to rub out,* and at other times ordinary criminals have launched synonyms for *to be executed, e.g., to fry, to take a hot squat* and *to walk the last mile* (electrocution), *to go up* and *to be topped* (hanging) and *to be gassed* (lethal gas). There are also many more decorous terms in the field of mortality; seldom encountered of late in city newspapers but still flourishing in the country weeklies are: *breathed his last, called home, laid to rest, long home, the Grim Reaper* and *the Pale Horseman.*

# Interludes

# 5

Hemingway appears to talk about bullfighting and wine, but really discusses the art of writing. Gertrude Stein takes an idiosyncratic view of the nature of language. E. B. White and Wolcott Gibbs admonish us about some characteristic faults in our approaches to writing.

# ERNEST HEMINGWAY

THIS seems to have gotten away from bullfighting, but the point was that a person with increasing knowledge and sensory education may derive infinite enjoyment from wine, as a man's enjoyment of the bullfight might grow to become one of his greatest minor passions, yet a person drinking, not tasting or savoring but *drinking*, wine for the first time will know, although he may not care to taste or be able to taste, whether he likes the effect or not and whether or not it is good for him. In wine, most people at the start prefer sweet vintages, Sauternes, Graves, Barsac, and sparkling wines, such as not too dry champagne and sparkling Burgundy because of their picturesque quality while later they would trade all these for a light but full and fine example of the Grand crus of Medoc though it may be in a plain bottle without label, dust, or cobwebs, with nothing picturesque, but only its honesty and delicacy and the light body of it on your tongue, cool in your mouth and warm when you have drunk it. So in bullfighting, at the start it is the picturesqueness of the paseo, the color, the scene, the picturesqueness of farols and molinetes, the bullfighter putting his hand on the muzzle of the bull, stroking the horns, and all such useless and romantic things that the spectators like. They are glad to see the horses protected if it saves them from awkward sights and they applaud all such moves. Finally, when they have learned to appreciate values through experience what they seek is honesty and true, not tricked, emotion and always classicism and the purity of execution of all the suertes, and, as in the change in taste for wines, they want no sweetening. . . .

[From the previously mentioned work, *Death in the Afternoon*.]

# GERTRUDE STEIN

WORDS have to do everything in poetry and prose and some writers write more in articles and prepositions and some say you should write in nouns, and of course one has to think of everything.

A noun is a name of anything, why after a thing is named write about it. A name is adequate or it is not. If it is adequate then why go on calling it, if it is not then calling it by its name does no good.

People if you like to believe it can be made by their names. Call anybody Paul and they get to be a Paul call anybody Alice and they get to be an Alice perhaps yes perhaps no, there is something in that, but generally speaking, things once they are named the name does not go on doing anything to them and so why write in nouns. Nouns are the name of anything and just naming names is alright when you want to call a roll but is it any good for anything else. To be sure in many places in Europe as in America they do like to call rolls.

As I say a noun is a name of a thing, and therefore slowly if you feel what is inside that thing you do not call it by the name by which it is known. Everybody knows that by the way they do when they are in love and a writer should always have that intensity of emotion about whatever is the object about which he writes. And therefore and I say it again more and more one does not use nouns.

Now what other things are there beside nouns, there are a lot of other things beside nouns.

When you are at school and learn grammar grammar is very exciting. I really do not know that anything has ever been more exciting than diagraming sentences. I suppose other things may be more exciting to others when they are at school but to me undoubtedly when I was at school the really completely exciting thing was diagraming sentences and that has been to me ever since

[From *Lectures in America*, by Gertrude Stein. Copyright 1935 and renewed 1962 by Alice B. Toklas. Reprinted by permission of Random House, Inc.]

146

the one thing that has been completely exciting and completely completing. I like the feeling the everlasting feeling of sentences as they diagram themselves.

In that way one is completely possessing something and incidentally one's self. Now in that diagraming of the sentences of course there are articles and prepositions and as I say there are nouns but nouns as I say even by definition are completely not interesting, the same thing is true of adjectives. Adjectives are not really and truly interesting. In a way anybody can know always has known that, because after all adjectives effect nouns and as nouns are not really interesting the thing that effects a not too interesting thing is of necessity not interesting. In a way as I say anybody knows that because of course the first thing that anybody takes out of anybody's writing are the adjectives. You see of yourself how true it is that which I have just said.

Beside the nouns and the adjectives there are verbs and adverbs. Verbs and adverbs are more interesting. In the first place they have one very nice quality and that is that they can be so mistaken. It is wonderful the number of mistakes a verb can make and that is equally true of its adverb. Nouns and adjectives never can make mistakes can never be mistaken but verbs can be so endlessly, both as to what they do and how they agree or disagree with whatever they do. The same is true of adverbs.

In that way any one can see that verbs and adverbs are more interesting than nouns and adjectives.

Beside being able to be mistaken and to make mistakes verbs can change to look like themselves or to look like something else, they are, so to speak on the move and adverbs move with them and each of them find themselves not at all annoying but very often very much mistaken. That is the reason any one can like what verbs can do. Then comes the thing that can of all things be most mistaken and they are prepositions. Prepositions can live one long life being really being nothing but absolutely nothing but mistaken and that makes them irritating if you feel that way about mistakes but certainly something that you can be continuously using and everlastingly enjoying. I like prepositions the best of all, and pretty soon we will go more completely into that.

Then there are articles. Articles are interesting just as nouns and adjectives are not. And why are they interesting just as nouns and adjectives are not. They are interesting because they do what a noun might do if a noun was not so unfortunately so completely unfortunately the name of something. Articles please, a and an and the please as the name that follows cannot please. They the names that is the nouns cannot please, because after all you know well after all that is what Shakespeare meant when he talked about a rose by any other name.

I hope now no one can have any illusion about a noun or about the adjective that goes with the noun.

But an article an article remains as a delicate and a varied something and any one who wants to write with articles and knows how to use them will always have the pleasure that using something that is varied and alive can give. That is what articles are.

Beside that there are conjunctions, and a conjunction is not varied but it has a force that need not make any one feel that they are dull. Conjunctions have made themselves live by their work. They work and as they work they live and even when they do not work and in these days they do not always live by work still nevertheless they do live.

So you see why I like to write with prepositions and conjunctions and articles and verbs and adverbs but not with nouns and adjectives. If you read my writing you will you do see what I mean.

Of course then there are pronouns. Pronouns are not as bad as nouns because in the first place practically they cannot have adjectives go with them. That already makes them better than nouns.

Then beside not being able to have adjectives go with them, they of course are not really the name of anything. They represent some one but they are not its or his name. In not being his or its or her name they already have a greater possibility of being something than if they were as a noun is the name of anything. Now actual given names of people are more lively than nouns which are the name of anything and I suppose that this is because after all the name is only given to that person when they are born, there is at least the element of choice even the element of change and anybody can be pretty well able to do what they like, they may be born Walter and become Hub, in such a way they are not like a noun. A noun has been the name of something for such a very long time.

That is the reason that slang exists it is to change the nouns which have been names for so long. I say again. Verbs and adverbs and articles and conjunctions and prepositions are lively because they all do something and as long as anything does something it keeps alive.

\*
\*
\*

Sentences and paragraphs. Sentences are not emotional but paragraphs are. I can say that as often as I like and it always remains as it is, something that is.

I said I found this out first in listening to Basket my dog drinking. And anybody listening to any dog's drinking will see what I mean.

# E. B. WHITE

A PUBLISHER in Chicago has sent us a pocket calculating machine by which we may test our writing to see whether it is intelligible. The calculator was developed by General Motors, who, not satisfied with giving the world a Cadillac, now dream of bringing perfect understanding

[From *The Second Tree from the Corner* (1954) by E. B. White: "Calculating Machine." Copyright 1951 by E. B. White. Reprinted by permission of Harper & Row, Publishers, and Hamish Hamilton Ltd.]

to men. The machine (it is simply a celluloid card with a dial) is called the Reading-Ease Calculator and shows four grades of "reading ease"—Very Easy, Easy, Hard, and Very Hard. You count your words and syllables, set the dial, and an indicator lets you know whether anybody is going to understand what you have written. An instruction book came with it, and after mastering the simple rules we lost no time in running a test on the instruction book itself, to see how *that* writer was doing. The poor fellow! His leading essay, the one on the front cover, tested Very Hard.

Our next step was to study the first phrase on the face of the calculator: "How to test Reading-Ease of written matter." There is, of course, no such thing as reading ease of written matter. There is the ease with which matter can be read, but that is a condition of the reader, not of the matter. Thus the inventors and distributors of this calculator get off to a poor start, with a Very Hard instruction book and a slovenly phrase. Already they have one foot caught in the brier patch of English usage.

Not only did the author of the instruction book score badly on the front cover, but inside the book he used the word "personalize" in an essay on how to improve one's writing. A man who likes the word "personalize" is entitled to his choice, but we wonder whether he should be in the business of giving advice to writers. "Whenever possible," he wrote, "personalize your writing by directing it to the reader." As for us, we would as lief Simonize our grandmother as personalize our writing.

In the same envelope with the calculator, we received another training aid for writers—a booklet called "How to Write Better," by Rudolf Flesch. This, too, we studied, and it quickly demonstrated the broncolike ability of the English language to throw whoever leaps cocksurely into the saddle. The language not only can toss a rider but knows a thousand tricks for tossing him, each more gay than the last. Dr. Flesch stayed in the saddle only a moment or two. Under the heading "Think Before You Write," he wrote, "The main thing to consider is your *purpose* in writing. Why are you sitting down to write?" And Echo answered: Because, sir, it is more comfortable than standing up.

Communication by the written word is a subtler (and more beautiful) thing than Dr. Flesch or General Motors imagines. They contend that the "average reader" is capable of reading only what tests Easy, and that the writer should write at or below this level. This is a presumptuous and degrading idea. There is no average reader, and to reach down toward this mythical character is to deny that each of us is on the way up, is ascending. ("Ascending," by the way, is a word Dr. Flesch advises writers to stay away from. Too unusual.)

It is our belief that no writer can improve his work until he discards the dulcet notion that the reader is feebleminded, for writing is an act of faith, not a trick of grammar. Ascent is at the heart of the matter. A country whose writers are following a calculating machine downstairs is not ascending—if you will pardon the expression—and a writer who questions the capacity of the person at the other end of the line is not a writer at all, merely a schemer. The movies long ago decided that a wider communication could be achieved by a deliberate descent to a lower level, and they walked proudly down until they reached the cellar. Now they are groping for the light switch, hoping to find the way out.

We have studied Dr. Flesch's instructions diligently, but we return for guidance in these matters to an earlier American, who wrote with more patience, more confidence. "I fear chiefly," he wrote, "lest my expression may not be extra-vagant enough, may not wander far enough beyond the narrow limits of my daily experience, so as to be adequate to the truth of which I have been convinced. . . . Why level downward to our dullest perception always, and praise that as common sense? The commonest sense is the sense of men asleep, which they express by snoring."

Run that through your calculator! It may come out Hard, it may come out Easy. But it will come out whole, and it will last forever.

# WOLCOTT GIBBS

THE average contributor to this magazine is semi-literate; that is, he is ornate to no purpose, full of senseless and elegant variations, and can be relied on to use three sentences where a word would do. It is impossible to lay down any exact and complete formula for bringing order out of this underbrush, but there are a few general rules.

1. Writers always use too damn many adverbs. On one page recently I found eleven modifying the verb "said." "He said morosely, violently, eloquently, so on." *Editorial theory should probably be that a writer who can't make his context indicate the way his character is talking ought to be in another line of work.* Anyway, it is impossible for a character to go through all these emotional states one after the other. Lon Chaney might be able to do it, but he is dead.

2. Word "said" is O.K. Efforts to avoid repetition by inserting "grunted," "snorted," etc., are waste motion and offend the pure in heart.

3. Our writers are full of clichés, just as old barns are full of bats. There is obviously no rule about this, except that anything that you suspect of being a cliché undoubtedly is one and had better be removed.

4. Funny names belong to the past or to whatever is left of *Judge* magazine. Any character called Mrs. Middlebottom of Joe Zilch should be summarily changed to something else. This goes for animals, towns, the names of imaginary books and many other things.

5. Our employer, Mr. Ross, has a prejudice against having too many sentences beginning with "and" or "but." He claims that they are conjunctions and should not be used purely for literary effect. Or at least only very judiciously. . . .

12. In the transcription of dialect, don't let the boys and girls misspell words just for a fake Bowery effect. There is no point, for instance, in "trubble," or "sed."

[From "Theory and Practice of Editing *New Yorker* Articles," quoted by James Thurber in *The Years with Ross*.]

13. Mr. Weekes said the other night, in a moment of desperation, that he didn't believe he could stand any more triple adjectives. "A tall, florid and overbearing man called Jaeckel." Sometimes they're necessary, but when every noun has three adjectives connected with it, Mr. Weekes suffers and quite rightly.

14. I suffer myself very seriously from writers who divide quotes for some kind of ladies' club rhythm.

"I am going," he said, "downtown" is a horror, and unless a quote is pretty long I think it ought to stay on one side of the verb. Anyway, it ought to be divided logically, where there would be pause or something in the sentence. . . .

18. I almost forgot indirection, which probably maddens Mr. Ross more than anything else in the world. He objects, that is, to important objects or places or people being dragged into things in a secretive and underhanded manner. If, for instance, a profile has never told where a man lives, Ross protests against a sentence saying, "His Vermont house is full of valuable paintings." Should say "He has a house in Vermont and it is full, etc." Rather weird point, but it will come up from time to time. . . .

20. The more "As a matter of facts," "howevers," "for instances," etc. etc. you can cut out, the nearer you are to the Kingdom of Heaven. . . .

29. Some of our writers are inclined to be a little arrogant about their knowledge of the French language. Probably best to put them back into English if there is a common English equivalent.

30. So far as possible make the pieces grammatical— but if you don't the copy room will, which is a comfort. Fowler's *English Usage* is our reference book. But don't be precious about it.

# Herbert Read

## FROM *ENGLISH PROSE STYLE*

The only thing that is indispensable for the possession of
a good style is personal sincerity. A sincere mind can and
does reject facts which do not fit into its hypotheses. The
lines of effective reasoning are as unlimited as the possible
constructions that a well-informed and facile mind can
place on events. Those who would persuade us of the
truth of a statement must rely, not on an air of conviction
or a show of reason, but on the compelling force of an
emotional attitude. The only way of judging these emotional attitudes is by the historical method; bad emotional
attitudes are shown up by their practical effects. Because
such attitudes are usually vague, prejudiced and personal,
some philosophers have thought that it would be well to
rely on open dogmas, however arbitrary these dogmas
might seem to critical minds.

Reasoning that depended entirely on true knowledge
would form a closed circle. It would be impossible to break
the chain of reasoning at any point and say, here is an
unresolved factor. Everything should be, in the words of
Sir Henry Maine, "lucidity, simplicity and system". Works
which fulfil this ideal are necessarily very rare; they
demand both aesthetic sensibility and a scientific temper.

\*
\*
\*

Words are the units of composition, and the art of
Prose must begin with a close attention to their quality. It
may be said that most bad styles are to be traced to a

[From *English Prose Style* by Sir Herbert Read. Reprinted by
permission of G. Bell & Sons, Ltd., London, and by Pantheon
Books, a division of Random House.]

neglect of this consideration; and certainly if style is reduced in the last analysis to a selective instinct, this instinct manifests itself most obviously in the use of words.

\*
\*
\*

In Prose the primary function of the sound of the isolated word is its expressiveness. It must *mean* the thing it stands for, not only in the logical sense of accurately corresponding to the intention of the writer but also in the visual sense of conjuring up a reflection of the thing in its completest reality.

\*
\*
\*

After sound, the quality of words is most determined by their *associations*. By their continued use in a certain connection words acquire an emotional surcharge of connotation which it is difficult to avoid in contexts where the simple use is intended. Such words are usually descriptive of events or situations which give rise to an excess of emotion or enthusiasm. By their continued association with these excesses, the words are in danger of meaning the excessive state and not the original content, which was determined by an objective and dispassionate use. *Love, death, soul, god, heart, poetic, little, sweet, quaint, passionate, mystic magic,* are all words which must be approached warily, if a vulgar or sentimental use of them is to be avoided. The words "love" and "hearts" in a passage like the following are not used with any definite connotation, but as hypnotic syllables which have only to be used "lavishly" enough to evoke vague romantic sentiments in the minds for which they are designed:

On a morning like this, with a world full of flowers and singing birds, and a heart full of love (and yet, by a unique paradox, hungry as ever for the love of a slip of a boy with big black eyes and crow-black blackness of hair and skilful hands and a heart overflowing with tenderness, a heart that had given love lavishly as it had received it) Amaryllis stood studying the situation. She did not exactly see how she could be surfeited with love and hungry for love at the same time. She only knew that she was. For one minute she could not think of a thing more to do for the little house of John Guido. . . .

GENE STRATTON-PORTER, *The Magic Garden.*

The surcharge of such words is not always base. There are words that have a magic ring of circumstance which no use can soil, as *honour, glory, courage, victory.* The difficulty in the use of these words is that they require a certain elevation of thought to give them their appropriate setting; and to attempt this elevation without the right equipment of mind and emotion is to risk bathos.

Apart from their sound and association, the choice of words is mainly governed by their *currency* and *congruity.* The state of a language is never constant, and almost every year words lose their life, and new words are born. To be aware of these subtle changes in the growth of a language requires the finest sensibility, and is perhaps peculiarly difficult for those who confine themselves to the reading of classical models. The vitality of writing corresponds in some inexorable way to its contemporaneity, and is nourished not so much by the study of examples, as by the act of living, from which it takes an accent of reality. The history of a word is entirely irrelevant in prose style: its face-value in current usage is the only criterion.

\*
\*
\*

. . . As Fenollosa makes clear, in prose it is not so much the presence or absence of the verb that matters, but the choice between a transitive and an intransitive verb. The great strength of the English language, he points out, "lies in its splendid array of transitive verbs, drawn both from Anglo-Saxon and from Latin sources. . . . Their power lies in their recognition of nature as a vast storehouse of forces. . . . I had to discover for myself why Shakespeare's English was so immeasurably superior to all others. I found that it was his persistent, natural, and magnificent use of hundreds of transitive verbs. Rarely will you find an "is" in his sentences. . . . A study of Shakespeare's verbs should underline all exercises in style."

Sentences in their variety run from simplicity to complexity, a progress not necessarily reflected in length: a long sentence may be extremely simple in construction—indeed, *must be* simple if it is to convey its sense easily.

Other things being equal, a series of short sentences will convey an impression of speed, and are therefore suited to the narration of action or historical events; whilst longer sentences give an air of solemnity and deliberation to writing.

\*
\*
\*

A noun substantive stands in an undivided empire of meaning, but it is an empire whose boundaries are undefined. Hardly a sentence passes but it is necessary to delimit or extend the meaning of a noun; and this we do by linking to it an epithet, that is, an adjectival word or phrase: *a man, many men, a good man, a black man,* are simple illustrations of various degrees of definition.

*Man* is no doubt an abstraction, built up of many particular events and acts of perception; but there is a limitation in this very abstraction; a vague but ready image is present in the mind, ready to be particularized by some concrete epithet. To say *a man* is merely to conjure up our own private idea of the typical man, perhaps a man in a black coat, striped trousers and a bowler hat, or perhaps the ideal athlete of Greek sculpture, or anything between these two extremes. To add an epithet implying an abstract quality like goodness scarcely makes any difference to our image; and this is the simple reason why such epithets are to be suspected of redundancy. To add a numerical epithet like *many* either multiplies the image in its indefiniteness, or creates another indefinite image of quantity, that is, *many men* is equivalent to *a crowd.* But to add an epithet of *quality* is to progress from the abstract and therefore unvisualized entity of *substance* to the definite entity of a *sense perception.* And since this is a progress from vagueness to vividness, it suggests that clear definition is an elementary need in prose style. But not all substantives are vague; and of epithets, not all that are appropriate are necessary. Indeed, we shall consider epithets under these two heads: namely, their Necessity and their Appropriateness.

A loose orotundity leads to the insertion of unnecessary attributes. It might seem to a novice that to introduce as many words as have a bearing on the subject must necessarily enlighten it. But as Congreve said (*Amendments of Mr. Collier's False and Imperfect Citations*), "epithets are beautiful in poetry, but make prose languishing and cold". *A man crossed the street* is a definite statement, vivid enough. To say *a man in black crossed the busy street* is to lose a certain immediateness of effect; for unless the context of the statement requires a man "in black" and a "busy" street, definitely for the furtherance of the narrative, then the understanding is merely delayed by the necessity of affixing these attributes to the general terms; for men are often enough in black, and streets busy. To say *a man in scarlet crossed the deserted street* is indeed to add to the vividness of the phrase; but these exceptional epithets, "scarlet" and "deserted", would never be used unless demanded by the context.

\*
\*
\*

The general rule is: to omit all epithets that may be assumed, and to admit only those which definitely further action, interest or meaning.

The bad effect of unnecessary epithets can only be adequately illustrated by giving a passage of prose, and then repeating it with the unnecessary epithets omitted.

Shining serenely as some immeasurable mirror beneath the smiling face of heaven, the solitary ocean lay in unrippled silence. It was in those placid latitudes south of the line in the Pacific, where weeks, aye months, often pass without the marginless blue level being ruffled by any wandering keel. Here, in almost perfect security from molestation by man, the innumerable denizens of the deep pursue their never-ending warfare, doubtless enjoying to the full the brimming cup of life, without a weary moment, and with no dreary anticipations of an unwanted old age.

Now it fell on a day that the calm surface of that bright sea was broken by the sudden upheaval of a compact troop of sperm whales from the inscrutable depths wherein they had been roaming and recruiting their gigantic energies upon the abundant molluscs, hideous of mien and insatiable of maw, that, like creations of a diseased mind, lurked far below the sunshine. The school consisted of seven cows and one mighty bull, who was unique in appearance, for instead of being in colour the unrelieved sepia common to his kind, he was curiously mottled with creamy white, making the immense oblong cube of his head look like a weather-worn monolith of Siena marble. Easeful as an Arabian khalif, he lolled supine upon the glittering folds of his couch, the welcoming wavelets caressing his vast form with gentlest touch, and murmuring softly as by their united efforts they rocked him in rhythm with their melodic lullaby.

FRANK T. BULLEN, *A Sack of Shakings*, pp. 1-2.

If we analyse this passage we shall find many super-fluous epithets or phrases; for examples

*serenely as* is duplicated by *placid*

*smiling* is perhaps permissible, but facetious

*solitary* is implied in the following sentence

*unrippled*: a mirror is never rippled

*weeks, aye*: nothing is lost by saying simply *months*

*marginless*: not necessary after immeasurable

*almost secure* is better, because shorter, than *in almost perfect security*

*by man*: molestation here implies "by man"

*denizens of the deep*: poetic *cliché*

*never-ending*: inexact, and therefore unnecessary, and even implied in *without a weary moment*.

*doubtless . . . cup of life*: a presumptuous cliché, irrelevant, if not contradictory to the idea of warfare

*dreary*: prevented by the absence of weary moments

*Now it fell on a day that*: *One day* expresses the meaning

*calm*: already implied

*compact*: a troop implies compactness

160

*inscrutable*: to whom? Not to the whales, and there is no one else on the scene

*abundant*: perhaps permissible, but not strictly necessary

*hideous . . . maw*: a cliché phrase destroying the effect of the following simile

*supine*: a whale cannot loll in any other position

*welcoming:* this is objectionable as a ludicrous personification of inanimate forces, but it is also to some extent duplicated by *caressing*

*softly*: implied in *murmuring,* but perhaps permissible in the sense of *sweetly.*

*melodic*: implied in *lullaby.*

There are other stylistic defects in this passage, particularly an almost constant use of *clichés,* and, indeed, the whole passage is one distended *cliché.* But neglecting these, and omitting only the redundant epithets in the above list, with a few consequent modifications of syntax, the passage then gains greatly in force, directness and expressiveness.

Shining like some immeasurable mirror beneath the face of heaven, the ocean lay in silence. It was in those placid latitudes south of the line in the Pacific, where months often pass without the blue level being ruffled by any wandering keel. Here, almost secure from molestation, the innumerable inhabitants of the sea pursue their warfare without a weary moment and with no anticipations of an unwanted old age.

One day the surface of that bright sea was broken by the sudden upheaval of a troop of sperm whales from the depths wherein they had been roaming and recruiting their gigantic energies upon the molluscs that, like creations of a diseased mind, lurked far below the sunshine. The school consisted of seven cows and one mighty bull, who was unique in appearance, for instead of being in colour the unrelieved sepia common to his kind, he was curiously mottled with creamy white, making the immense oblong cube of his head look like a weather-worn monolith of Siena marble. Easeful as any Arabian khalif he lolled upon the glittering folds of his couch, the wavelets caressing his vast form and murmuring softly as by their united efforts they rocked him in rhythm with their lullaby.

Fifty words have been saved, but nothing essential has been taken from the meaning, whilst the force and "activity" of the writing is all the greater for the lifting of this unnecessary burden of epithets.

\*
\*
\*

The use of symbols in an exact and consistent way is the foundation of unequivocal expression, and therefore of good prose. Good prose is not confined to unequivocal expression: it also has emotive uses . . . . But good expository prose is the organization of symbols into a structure which we call *reasoning*. . . . Reasoning is . . . the reference of detached observations to a general background of knowledge, with the result that these observations can be brought into a mutual relationship and therefore into a unity of argument by the all-embracing resources of this background. And this fact it is which gives to reasoning that coherence and movement which is directly reflected in the quality of the style.

\*
\*
\*

The sense of the quality of words; the use of appropriate epithets and images; the organization of the period, the paragraph and the plot; the arts of exposition and of narrative; all the gifts of thought and sensibility—these are only dry perfections unless they are moved by a spirit which is neither intelligence nor emotion, but the sustained power of reason. And by reason in this context I do not mean ratiocination or rationality, but, as I have said in another connection, 'the widest evidence of the senses, and of all processes and instincts developed in the history of man. It is the sum total of awareness, ordained and ordered to some specific end or object of attention'. Such a quality in a writer is no innate instinct, but a conscious achievement. It is more than character, because it necessarily implies intelligence; and it is more

162

than personality, because it necessarily implies a realm of absolute ideals. A life of reason is more than a life of self-development, because it is also a life of self-devotion, of service to outer and autocratic abstractions.

This is merely to say that a good style is not the making of a great writer; and the corollary is, that a great writer is always a good stylist. The greatest English prose writers Swift, Milton, Taylor, Hooker, Berkeley, Shelley, are great not only by virtue of their prose style, but also by virtue of the profundity of their outlook on the world. And these are not separable and distinct virtues, but two aspects of one reality. The thought seems to mould and accentuate the style, and the style reacts to mould and accentuate the thought. It is one process of creation, one art, one aim.

*<br>*<br>*

. . . The writer should convey to the reader the *speed* of events, and the *actuality* of objects. Both these effects are best secured by economy of expression: that is to say, the words used to convey the impression should be just sufficient. If there are too many words, the action is clogged, the actuality blurred. If too few, the impression is not conveyed in its completeness; the outlines are vague. In either case there is a lack of visual clarity.

These rules seem obvious, but they have seldom been observed, and good narrative writing is comparatively rare in English literature. There is a human failing which urges us to elaborate and decorate our descriptions; it is perhaps merely the desire to infuse an objective activity with something of the personality of the narrator. There is, too, the irresistible attraction of words in themselves, urging us to use them for their own sakes rather than as exact symbols of the things they stand for. With these various dangers waylaying him, the writer can rarely exercise sufficient restraint to enable him to keep his eye on the object, and give to the reader the concreteness of the things he perceives. But if the eye should *distort* what it sees, and give a fictitious vitality to things that are really lifeless, the reader will begin to feel uneasy. The following paragraph from the beginning of Rudyard Kipling's *Love-o'-Women* is worth consideration from this point of view:

> The horror, the confusion, and the separation of the murderer from his comrades were all over before I came. There remained only on the barrack-square the blood of man calling from the ground. The hot sun had dried it to a dusky goldbeater-skin film, cracked lozenge-wise by the heat; and as the wind rose, each lozenge, rising a little, curled up at the edges as if it were a dumb tongue. Then a heavier gust blew all away down wind in grains of dark-coloured dust. It was too hot to stand in the sunshine before breakfast. The men were in barracks talking the matter over. A knot of soldiers' wives stood by one of the entrances to the married quarters, while inside a woman shrieked and raved with wicked filthy words.
>
> RUDYARD KIPLING, *Many Inventions*, p. 261.

We can readily admit that an accent of violence was needed and is very effective at the outset of this story, and that the heat of the tropical sun must be conveyed to the reader. But a melodramatic phrase like "the blood of man" gives a warning that all is *not* well. "A dusky goldbeater-skin film" is excellent; we see that film and can see it cracking lozenge-wise in the heat. But then the vision gets distorted. The "dumb tongues" are not eloquent; merely stage properties. And did the author really see those grains of dark-coloured dust which a heavier gust blew all away? There is, admittedly, an effective device in prose style which we might call "the microscopic eye". . . . Here, however, there is no distortion, but a minute and precise observation.

We find the best narrative prose in ages when the epic spirit has prevailed, that is to say, in writers who have been more conscious of their theme than of their own feelings and opinions. The narrative is essentially addressed to an audience: it is not a self-revelation or a self-expression. It is accurate reporting. It is therefore devoid of comment and the only point of view it represents is the point of view of an interested observer.

*
*
*

*Constructional arrangement* is either a logical arrangement of units of an intuitive character, such as may be required for the selection and ordering of a volume of essays or short stories; or it is an arrangement of logical thought in such a manner that the structure of the composition reflects the order and sequence of the thinking. . . . Such a structure must be completed before the actual writing of the treatise is begun. It is a preliminary ordering of material, so as to make the most effective use of that material—to avoid repetitions and redundancies, to secure the presentation of arguments in their due sequence, to work up to a climax in the argument, and to bring home the conclusion clearly and at a timely moment. The "Contents" list of any great didactic work, such as the *Summa Theologica* of St. Thomas Aquinas, the *Ethics* of Spinoza, or the *Ecclesiastical Polity* of Hooker, will admirably illustrate this skeleton structure.

The perfection of a structure of this kind secures the logical arrangement of ideas and so preserves the unity of the thesis; without such a logical framework, irrelevant matter might be introduced under cover of some passing association of ideas; the wild goose and the red herring are common pests in logical writing, and nets must be constructed to exclude them.

*
*
*

This insistence on a unity of approach, on a coherence of plan, on an ordering of material—is a salutary exhortation, and not intended as an encouragement to the roundheads of literature. Once the plan is made and the material parcelled out, then the dry skeleton of this structure should be hidden beneath a surface which is all variety and interest. And that, of course, is the virtue of a good style. It intervenes between the bare structures of the intellect and those regions of the mind which are only open to sensuous perceptions.

*
*
*

Rhythm is not an *a priori* construction. It is not an ideal form to which we fit our words. Above all it is not a musical notation to which our words submit.

Rhythm is more profound than this. It is born, not with the words, but with the thought, and with whatever confluence of instincts and emotions the thought is accompanied. As the thought takes shape in the mind, it takes *a* shape. It has always been recognized that clear thinking precedes good writing. There is about good writing a visual actuality. It exactly reproduces what we should metaphorically call the contour of our thought. The metaphor is for once exact: thought has a contour of shape. The paragraph is the perception of this contour or shape.

The writer has towards his materials, words, the same relation that an artist, say a modeller, has towards his material, clay. The paragraph is a plastic mass, and it takes its shape from the thought it has to express: its shape *is* the thought.

This is the distinction between a dead paragraph and a living paragraph: in the first case a writer's words flow until either a phase of his logic is complete, or the simulated oratory of his periods demands a pause, or for no reason whatsoever; but in the second case the words rise like clay on the potter's wheel: the downward force of attention, or concentration, or intuition, and the driving force of emotion or feeling—between these forces the words rise up, take shape, become a complete pattern a "good" *gestalt*.

*
*
*

. . . The paragraph is, indeed, the first complete and independent unit of prose rhythm. The sentence has rhythm, but as we have seen, a prose all sentences, even if these are in themselves perfectly rhythmical, is not perfect prose. The sentences must be dissolved in a wider movement and this wider movement is the rhythm of the paragraph—a rhythm that begins with the first syllable of the paragraph and is not complete without the last syllable. With the last syllable the rhythm ends and there is a rest.

The rhythmical unity of the paragraph may be a unity of actual composition: compare Gibbon's conscious practice (the conscious practice of many writers, but perhaps more often an unconscious instinct)—

"It has always been my practice to cast a long paragraph in a single mould, to try it by my ear, to deposit it in my memory, but to suspend the action of the pen till I had given the last polish to my work."—*Autobiography*.

Rhythm in this sense may be no more than "an instinct for the difference between what sounds right and what sounds wrong" (Fowler: *Modern English Usage*). This might be still a question of "ear", but Wimsatt . . . holds that prose rhythm is a matter of emphasis; it is putting the important words where they sound important. It is a matter of coherence; it is putting the right idea in the right place." It would follow, as Wimsatt recognizes, that we should not properly speak of rhythm at all in relation to prose—" 'Rhythm,' when used literally, means 'measure' or 'regularity', and since the movement of good prose is precisely *not* regular but varied with the sense, the union of the terms 'prose' and 'rhythm' has been none of the happiest."

\*
\*
\*

Metaphor is the swift illumination of an equivalence. Two images, or an idea and an image, stand equal and opposite; clash together and respond significantly, surprising the reader with a sudden light.

This light may either illuminate or decorate the sentence in which it is found; and perhaps we may divide all metaphors into the *illuminative* and the *decorative*. By doing so we can make more distinct the limited relevance

167

of metaphor to prose writing; for while both kinds are appropriate to poetry, only the illuminative metaphor will be found appropriate in pure prose style.

*
*
*

The language of scientific pioneers like Faraday, Darwin and Huxley abounds in illuminative metaphors. Here, for example, is a paragraph from the work of a modern physicist:

I have said that all atoms are in motion, and that there is a constant struggle between some form of attractive force which would draw all the atoms together and this motion which would keep them independent. The existence of an attractive force which we here take into account as something very important does not at first seem to be reconcilable with the atomic structure we have just considered, because in this we supposed that the outer shells of electrons would prevent the atoms from coming too close to each other. It is a difficult point, because both views are entirely correct. It is, no doubt, our present ignorance of the nature of these forces that prevents us from arriving at a clear understanding. We have seen how it can happen that when two atoms approach each other at great speeds they go through one another, while at moderate speeds they bound off each other like two billiard balls. We have to go a step further, and see how, at very slow speeds of approach, they may actually stick together. We have all seen those swinging gates which when their swing is considerable, go to and fro without locking. When the swing has declined, however, the latch suddenly drops into its place, the gate is held and after a short rattle the motion is all over. We have to explain an effect something like that. When the two atoms meet, the repulsions of their electron shells usually cause them to recoil; but if the motion is small, and the atoms spend a longer time in each other's neighbourhood, there is time for something to happen in the internal arrangements of both atoms, like the drop of the latch-gate into its socket, and the atoms are held. It all depends on some structure of the atom which causes a want of uniformity over its surface, so that there is usually a repulsion; but the repulsion will be turned into attraction if the two atoms are allowed time to make the necessary arrangements, or even if at the outset they are presented to each other in the right way.

Sir William Bragg: *Concerning the Nature of Things*

The following passage shows the use of merely decorative metaphors:

The Oxford Movement may be a spent wave, but, before it broke on the shore, it reared, as its successor is now rearing, a brave and beautiful crest of liturgical and devotional life, the force of which certainly shifted the Anglican sands, though it failed to uncover any rock-bottom underlying them. It is enough if now and then a lone swimmer be borne by the tide, now at its full, to be dashed, more or less ungently, upon the Rock of Peter, to cling there in safety, while the impotent wave recedes and is lost in the restless sea.

M. A. Chapman, in *Blackfriars*, April, 1921
(Quoted by Stephen J. Brown, *The World of Imagery*, p. 308)

# *Interludes*

# *6*

Thurber contributes another anecdote about his ir-
ritable editor. Pound gives advice on ways to teach
students a good prose style. Churchill tells us about
learning to write.

# JAMES THURBER

. . . ("There's that goddam 'pretty' again," Ross would say. The easy overuse of "pretty" and "little" exacerbated his uneasy mind. Once, to bedevil him, I used them both in a single sentence of a Talk piece: "The building is pretty ugly and a little big for its surroundings." After stumbling upon these deliberate oxymora, Ross poked his head into my office, made a pretty ugly sound with his tongue and lips, and withdrew. We had been discussing the goddam pretty-little problem earlier that same day.)

[This selection is from Thurber's *The Years with Ross*.]

# EZRA POUND

1. Let the pupils exchange composition papers and see how many and what useless words have been used—how many words that convey nothing new.

2. How many words that obscure the meaning.

3. How many words out of their usual place, and whether this alteration makes the statement in any way more interesting or more energetic.

4. Whether a sentence is ambiguous; whether it really means more than one thing or more than the writer intended; whether it can be so read as to mean something different.

5. Whether there is something clear on paper, but ambiguous if spoken aloud.

*
*
*

[These selections are from *The ABC of Reading* and *The Literary Essays*, respectively.]

Use no superfluous word, no adjective which does not reveal something.

Don't use such an expression as "dim lands *of peace.*" It dulls the image. It mixes an abstraction with the concrete. It comes from the writer's not realizing that the natural object is always the *adequate* symbol.

Go in fear of abstractions.

*<br>*<br>*

The problem of sentence structure was undeniably discussed during several centuries.

A carpenter can put boards together, but a good carpenter would know seasoned wood from green.

The mere questions of constructing and assembling clauses, of parsing and grammar are not enough. Such study ended in a game of oratory, now parodied in detective stories when they give the learned counsel's summing-up.

The development after these structural exercises occurred chiefly in France: Stendhal, Flaubert.

An attempt to set down things as they are, to find the word that corresponds to the thing, the statement that portrays, and presents, instead of making a comment, however brilliant, or an epigram.

*<br>*<br>*

Incompetence will show in the use of too many words.

The reader's first and simplest test of an author will be to look for words that do not function; that contribute nothing to the meaning OR that distract from the MOST important factor of the meaning to factors of minor importance.

*<br>*<br>*

Mr. Swinburne is famed or infamed for having used a great many which express nothing but "colour" or "splendour". It has been said that he used the same adjectives to describe a woman and a sunset.

# WINSTON CHURCHILL

. . . By being so long in the lowest form I gained an immense advantage over the cleverer boys. They all went on to learn Latin and Greek and splendid things like that. But I was taught English. We were considered such dunces that we could learn only English. Mr. Somervell—a most delightful man, to whom my debt is great—was charged with the duty of teaching the stupidest boys the most disregarded thing—namely, to write mere English. He knew how to do it. He taught it as no one else has ever taught it. Not only did we learn English parsing thoroughly, but we also practised continually English analysis. Mr. Somervell had a system of his own. He took a fairly long sentence and broke it up into its components by means of black, red, blue and green inks. Subject, verb, object: Relative Clauses, Conditional Clauses, Conjunctive and Disjunctive Clauses! Each had its colour and its bracket. It was a kind of drill. We did it almost daily. As I remained in the Third Fourth (B) three times as long as anyone else, I had three times as much of it. I learned it thoroughly. Thus I got into my bones the essential structure of the ordinary British sentence—which is a noble thing.

*
*
*

I had meanwhile been working continuously upon *The River War*. . . . I affected a combination of the styles of Macaulay and Gibbon, the staccato antitheses of the former and the rolling sentences and genitival endings of the latter; and I stuck in a bit of my own from time to time. I began to see that writing, especially narrative, was not only an affair of sentences, but of paragraphs. Indeed I thought the paragraph no less important than the sentence. Macaulay is a master of paragraphing. Just as the sentence contains one idea in all its fullness, so the paragraph should embrace a distinct epidsode; and as sentences should follow one another in harmonious sequence, so the paragraphs must fit on to one another like the automatic couplings of railway carriages. Chapterisation also began to dawn upon me. Each chapter must be self-contained. All the chapters should be of equal value and more or less of equal length. Some chapters define themselves naturally and obviously; but much more difficulty arises when a number of heterogeneous incidents none of which can be omitted have to be woven together into what looks like an integral theme. Finally the work must be surveyed as a whole and due proportion and strict order established from beginning to end. I already knew that chronology is the key to easy narrative. I already realised that "good sense is the foundation of good writing." I warned myself against the fault of beginning my story as some poor people do "Four thousand years before the Deluge," and I repeated earnestly one of my best French quotations, "L'art d'être ennuyeux, c'est de tout dire." I think I will repeat it again now.

# James Thurber

## THE NEW VOCABULARIANISM

A sensitive gentleman in one of Henry James's novels exclaims at the end, triumphantly, "Then there we are!" not because he and his fair companion have arrived at a solution of anything but because they have come upon an embraceable impasse.

The expression Embraceable Impasse (I stress it with capitals deliberately) might well become a part of the jargon of today's diplomacy, which so often seems content to settle for a phrase in place of a way out. One such phrase, Calculated Risk, has been going great guns among the politicians and statesmen. It was used repeatedly by an adult guest on an American radio discussion panel made up of juveniles. (I am glad and eager to announce that we have millions of teenagers in America more interested in using their minds than in brandishing knives or bicycle chains.) Finally one youth interrupted the adult to say "I don't know what you mean by Calculated Risk." The grown-up was as bewildered as if the youngster had said "I don't know whom you mean by Harry Truman." This particular Calculated Risk was being applied to the Russo-American plan of exchange students, and the adult guest floundered a bit in trying to explain what he meant.

Now I have made some study of the smoke-screen phrases of the political terminologists, and they have to be described rather than defined. Calculated Risk, then, goes like this: "We have every hope and assurance that the plan will be successful, but if it doesn't work we knew all the time it wouldn't, and said so."

There is, to be sure, a kind of menacing Alice in Wonderland meaninglessness in a great deal of modern political phraseology. What used to be called a tenable position could now often be called, quite fittingly, a Tenniel position. To add to the unmeaningfulness of it all, there is the continual confusing contribution of the abbreviationists. We have in America a product called No-Cal, short for No Calories, and another Decaf, meaning "coffee from which caffein has been removed." Before long, I fear, Calculated Risk will become Cal-Ris, and then all the other celebrated phrases will be abbreviated, for the sake of making even less sense than before in front-page headlines. We shall have to have a special glossary, perhaps, to help us figure out "Pea-Coex" and "Ag-Reapp" and "Mass-Retal." I should think even the most backward student of world affairs would understand "Sum-Con." Then the Marxist intellectuals will hit them with those old brickbats called Obscurantism and Obfuscationism. The meaning of these two words will be described, in my own forthcoming dictionary, like this: "You are seeking to distort our objectives by exposing them to the scrutiny of the unfairest of all bourgeois virtues, namely truth."

Somewhere in my proposed lexicon I shall have to wedge in what a lady said to me when I told her I was writing a short piece about the time, if any, of Man on earth. She said, with a distressed sigh, "So much has already been written about everything that you can't find out anything about it."

The brain of our species is, as we know, made up largely of potassium, phosphorus, propaganda, and politics, with the result that how not to understand what should be clearer is becoming easier and easier for all of us. Sanity, soundness, and sincerity, of which gleams and stains can still be found in the human brain under powerful microscopes, flourish only in a culture of clarification, which is now becoming harder and harder to detect with the naked eye. My dictionary, in attacking or circling about the terminology of the declarificationists, will contain such directives as this, for the bewildermentation of exchange students on all sides: "When you find that they are superior to us in any field, remember that their superiority is inferior to ours."

Let us mourn for a moment the death of Latin in American high schools. That ancient sword of Cicero, lyre of Catullus, and thunder of Virgil has become the pallid valet of the lawyer and the doctor, laying out their double-breasted polysyllabics, workaday clichés, and full-dress circumlocutions. "I had to let my secretary go," a doctor told me. "She could never remember the Latin for cod liver oil." In my day, Latin was taught in high schools to prepare the youthful mind for the endless war between meaning and gobbledegook. But it was a mental discipline, and discipline has become a bad word in America, for the idiotic reason that we identify it with regimentation, and hence damn it as Communistic. Recent surveys in my country indicate that Latin and certain other difficult subjects were eliminated from school curricula because they were simply too hard for Junior and his sister to understand, and interfered with the coziness of their security. An aroused America is now, I am glad to say, interested in the rehabilitation of our declining educational system. We have long had, in our colleges and unisities, easy courses variously known as snap, soft, cinch, and pudd, which seems to be short for "pudding." I asked a pretty girl graduate of the University of Kansas if she had taken any pudd courses, and she said she had taken two. Common Insect Pests and Native Shrubs and Trees. "They were so dull I failed them both," she told me.

The tendency of tired American businessmen and statesmen to use slang and slogan will, I hope, disappear with the revival of true education. When our recent President used the word "gimmick" for "political device" he seemed to open the door for a flood of Hollywood shibboleth. I can only pray that Washington does not fall into the use of "switcheroo" and "twisterino."

My concern about the precarious state of the English language in the hands or on the tongues of politicians shows up in recurring nightmares. I dreamed one night I was at some kind of Sum-Con, and two famous lines, one English, the other American, became garbled slightly and unfortunately conjoined. They were Browning's "Beautiful Evelyn Hope is dead," and that proud boast of all New England inns, "George Washington slept here." They came out in my nightmare like this: "Beautiful Evelyn Hope is deaf. George Washington slapt her."

"Gentlemen, this means war," said a grave voice in my dream, and I woke up. It was hard to get back to sleep, and I thought many thoughts. I began worrying again about the death of Latin, and I said aloud, waking up my wife, "What does he know of English who only English knows?" The restoration of Latin in our schools is not going to save Man from himself, to be sure, but it would help in the coming struggle for a world regime of sense and sanity. *Hoc est*, at any rate, *in votis*.

# Conclusions

Two of the greatest modern writers end this book
with advice which all of us—whether we are writing,
or reading, or simply taking our place in society—
can remember with profit for the rest of our lives.

ERNEST HEMINGWAY

# EZRA POUND

Let the pupil examine a given piece of writing, say, the day's editorial in a newspaper, to see whether the writer is trying to conceal something; to see whether he is "veiling his meaning"; whether he is afraid to say what he thinks; whether he is trying to appear to think without really doing any thinking.

[From *The ABC of Reading*.]


# ERNEST HEMINGWAY

. . . The great thing is to last and get your work done and see and hear and learn and understand; and write when there is something that you know; and not before; and not too damned much after. Let those who want to save the world if you can get to see it clear and as a whole. Then any part you make will represent the whole if it's made truly. The thing to do is work and learn to make it.

[From *Death in the Afternoon*.]

# Index

Abstraction
    Fowler, 81-82
    Pound, 62-63

Adjectives
    Fowler, 82-84
    Read, 158-162

Ambiguity (*see* Clarity)
    Graves and Hodge, 41-45

Clarity (general)
    Fowler, 113-114
    Graves and Hodge, 11-12
    Hemingway, 31-32
    Pound, 61-65, 75-76
    Read, 156

Clarity (organization)
    Churchill, 175-176
    Graves and Hodge, 44-50
    Read, 165-166
    Wilson, 67-72

Cliché (*see* Ready-Made
        Phrases)
    Fowler, 87-89
    Read, 161

Connotation
    Pound, 63-65
    Read, 156-157

Consistency of style
    Graves and Hodge, 52

Decoration
    Hemingway, 59
    Quiller-Couch, 76-77
    Simenon, 123-124
    Woolf, 58

Euphemism
    Fowler, 84-85
    Mencken, 127-142
    Orwell, 24

Example of bad style
    Orwell, 14-15, 20-21, 24
    Quiller-Couch, 77
    Wilson, 68-69, 71

Foreign words
    Orwell, 17-18

Jargon
    Fowler, 111-112
    Porter, 122-123
    Quiller-Couch, 77

Meaningless Words
 Orwell, 19-22

Metaphors
 Fowler, 97-98
 Graves and Hodge, 50-51
 Orwell, 16, 22
 Read, 167-169

Participles
 Fowler, 113

Passive construction
 Fowler, 102-103
 Orwell, 17
 Quiller-Couch, 77
 Read, 157-158

Premises of good style
 Gibbs, 152-153
 Graves and Hodge, 11-12,
  40-41
 Orwell, 22-23, 25-28
 Read, 162-163
 Woolf, 58

Prepositions
 Fowler, 104-107

Pretentious diction
 Fowler, 86-87, 93-97, 99,
  115-116
 Orwell, 17-18
 Simenon, 123-124

Quotations
 Fowler, 107-109

Ready-made phrases
 (*see* Cliché)
 Fowler, 89-93
 Orwell, 21

Repetition
 Graves and Hodge, 45-46

Rhythm
 Fowler, 109-111
 Read, 166-167

Sentence length
 Graves and Hodge, 52-54

Style as character
 Capote, 124-125
 Fowler, 111-112
 Frost, 57
 Hemingway, 59
 Marianne Moore, 123
 Porter, 121
 Pound, 75-76
 Quiller-Couch, 76
 Read, 155, 162-163
 Wilson, 67-72 *passim*
 Woolf, 58

Verb misuse
 Fowler, 98
 Orwell, 17

Vulgarization
 Fowler, 114-115

Wordiness
 Orwell, 17
 Pound, 174
 Read, 163-165
 White, 120

Writing and Society
 Graves and Hodge, 37-40
 Orwell, 13- *passim*
 Pound, 59-65